gifts to sew
for special occasions

gifts to sew
for special occasions

BETTERWAY BOOKS
CINCINNATI, OHIO

Front cover: (top left): Eaglemoss/Graham Rae,
(top centre, top right): Eaglemoss/Lizzie Orme,
(main): VNU/Baby & Peuter Magazine.

Page 3: VNU/Baby & Peuter Magazine,
page 5: Eaglemoss/George Taylor,
page 6: IPC Syndication
(Homes & Gardens/Marie-Louise Avery).

First published in North America
in 2000 by Betterway Books
an imprint of F&W Publications, Inc.
1507 Dana Avenue
Cincinnati, OH 45207
1-800/289-0963

ISBN 1-55870-575-9

Printed in Hong Kong

10 9 8 7 6 5 4 3 2 1

Contents

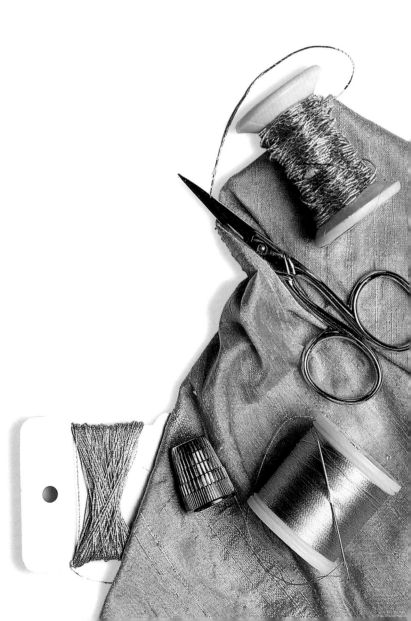

Lacy home accessories

Spoil the bride with feminine dressing-room accessories. Make a
tissue box cover, shoe tree covers, and scented heart-shaped sachets,
all lavishly trimmed with ribbon roses and lace.

These dainty accessories have a timeless appeal, created by layering lace on to fine cotton, linen or silk. Ribbon roses, bows and satin ribbon and binding contribute to the final look of each item. The covers and sachets are quite simple to make – it is the trimmings that create the effect.

You can trim the items in any way you fancy, so plunder your sewing basket for your favorite remnants of lace and ribbon. An exact color match between your chosen trimmings and the base fabric is not necessary – in fact, you will create a better effect if there are subtle differences between the two.

Use the very different textures of the lace, ribbons and background fabric as a design tool too, and make sure there are lots of rich, contrasting textures. For instance, if your lace is matte, use a silky fabric as the background, or introduce lush satin ribbons into the design.

▼ *The tissue box cover is topped with organza and a ribbon rose trimming. This type of trim is very versatile, as the ribbon roses can also be cut from the braid and used individually, as on the coordinating accessories.*

Making a tissue box cover

To create a charming heirloom look, choose a pale-colored fine fabric, such as cotton, linen or silk. Very few of these fabrics are completely opaque, so you usually need two layers to ensure they completely hide the item they are covering. With the tissue box cover, it helps if you choose a tissue box that is pale to start with. The method given can be used to cover a box of any shape.

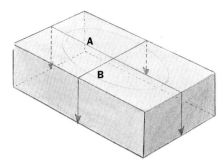

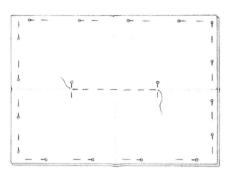

You will need

- ◆ Box of tissues
- ◆ Remnant of cream fabric
- ◆ Lace trimmings
- ◆ Satin ribbon for bows (optional)
- ◆ Ribbon roses (optional)
- ◆ Satin bias binding
- ◆ Matching sewing thread
- ◆ Tape measure
- ◆ Dressmaker's pencil
- ◆ Ruler
- ◆ Pins

1 Measuring the box Measure lengthways along the top of the tissue box and down each side (**A**). Then measure widthways along the top and down each side of the box (**B**). Draw two rectangles measuring **A** by **B** on the fabric and cut out.

2 Marking the opening Pin the fabric rectangles right sides together around the edges. To mark the center, fold the rectangle in quarters and press lightly along creases. Measure length of opening on tissue box. Use pins to mark this length centrally on longer pressed line; tack between the pins.

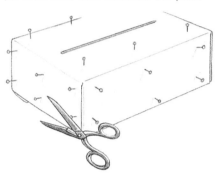

4 Turning the cover To turn the cover right side out, lift the upper layer of fabric and push it through the opening. Press, so the seamlines sit at the edges of the opening. Smooth the layers flat and tack together around the opening and the outer edges.

5 Fitting the cover Place the cover over the tissue box, pleating the fabric neatly at the corners so it fits smoothly round the box; secure in place with pins pushed into the box. If necessary, trim off any points of fabric protruding below the pleats.

▶ *This cover is simply a double-layered rectangle of ivory linen, bound at the edges. The sheen of the lace and the satin binding forms a pleasing contrast with the matte, textured linen.*

3 Stitching the opening Machine stitch 3mm (⅛in) either side of the tacked line, pivoting the fabric to stitch across each short end. Cut along the tacked line carefully and snip diagonally into the corners. Remove the pins.

6 Adding the lace Decide where to place the trimmings, lace and any bows and ribbon roses. Put the bows and ribbon roses to one side and pin the lace to hold. Remove the cover and machine or handstitch the lace in place. For deep picot lace, catch down the points with small handstitches.

7 Binding the edges Neaten the outer edges of the cover by binding them with satin bias binding.

8 Completing the cover Put the cover back on the tissue box. Re-fold the corner pleats and hold them in place with pins. Remove the cover and secure the pleats with small handstitches, worked on the inside of the cover. To finish the cover, handstitch the remaining bows and ribbon rose trims neatly in place.

Traceable pattern for heart sachet

Making a scented heart sachet

These romantic heart sachets, with a few pieces of fragrant dried lavender or potpourri mixed into the padding, will keep the bride's dresser drawers or dressing table smelling sweet.

You can make them from scraps of fabric, lace and ribbon trims. Use a firm, closely woven fabric or double layers of a finer fabric so that the padding and potpourri do not show through. For the padding, use old tights, batting or cotton balls, and mix in a little potpourri (avoid types which have large, scratchy pieces).

Making a sachet Use the traceable pattern for the heart sachet to cut two heart shapes. Hand or machine stitch the trims to the right side of one heart shape, then tack the hearts right sides together. Carefully machine stitch round the outer edges, taking a 6mm (¼in) seam allowance and leaving a small opening in one side for turning. Turn sachet to right side and press carefully, using a pressing cloth to protect delicate fabrics. Pad the heart, slipping some dried lavender or potpourri into the center. Slip stitch the opening closed.

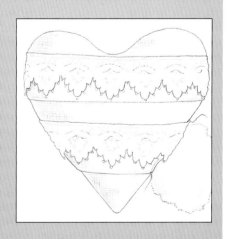

Shoe tree covers

The base of this design is a pair of plain, inexpensive velour shoe trees, sold by fabric stores and shoe shops. The small plastic handle, which is difficult to cover, is hidden by a deep lace frill. As with the tissue box cover, use up scraps and remnants of fabric and lace. Doubled fabric is used here too, to ensure that the color of the velour does not show through.

You will need

- ◆ **Pair of shoe trees**
- ◆ **Remnant of cream fabric**
- ◆ **Satin bias binding**
- ◆ **60cm (⅝yd) of lace, about 8cm (3in) wide**
- ◆ **Lace trimmings**
- ◆ **1.5m (1½yd) of double-sided satin ribbon**
- ◆ **Individual ribbon roses (optional)**
- ◆ **Matching sewing thread**
- ◆ **Pins**

1 Cutting out For each shoe tree, cut two 25 x 20cm (10 x 8in) rectangles of fabric. Tack the two rectangles wrong sides together around the edges.

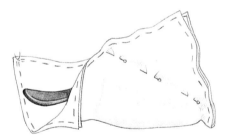

2 Fitting the cover Stretch the doubled fabric rectangle over the front of the tree, bringing the two short ends to meet on the underside; pin along top shaped area. Slip the fabric off the tree and stitch along the pinned line. Trim the seam allowances to 3mm (⅛in) and press them open. Turn the cover to the right side.

3 Binding the top edge Trim the top of the cover so it is straight. Bind the raw edge with satin bias binding.

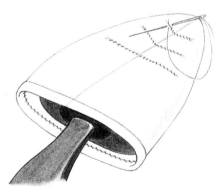

4 Shaping the cover Ease the cover back on to the tree. On the underside, pin small darts to take in the excess fabric. Catch the darts in place at the toe end of the tree with neat, firm handstitches.

5 Hiding the handle Cut the 8cm (3in) wide lace in half. Overlap raw edges to form a circle and pin. Set the sewing machine to a wide zigzag and stitch along the join. Work a row of gathering stitches along straight edge of lace, then pull up the gathers. Place the gathered edge round base of handle and tie off the thread ends.

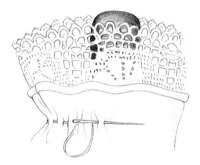

6 Securing the frill Working from the right side and using doubled thread, handstitch lace frill in place, gathering up the cover at the base of the handle at the same time. The stitches will be hidden by the ribbon.

7 Trimming the cover Handstitch lace on to the cover, as desired. Tie a ribbon bow around the top and secure it at the center with a few neat stitches. To prevent the ends of the bow being caught when the tree is used, take them to the underside of the tree and slip stitch them down. If you like, stitch a small ribbon rose to the center of the bow.

Small drawstring bags

Using a simple drawstring design, you can make a glamorous evening bag, a pretty little bag for a bridesmaid to carry or handy storage bags that look good enough to display in the home.

Apart from your basic sewing kit, all you need to make these dainty drawstring bags is a remnant of fabric plus some cord or ribbon for the drawstring. Such bags are the perfect reason for hunting out that piece of plush velvet or sparkling brocade you've hoarded away for ages so that you can turn it into a swish evening accessory. They are also a good excuse to make country-style storage bags from odd scraps of checked and floral cottons.

The style described here is a full bag gathered on to a circular base. But you could choose a simpler style made from two rectangles of fabric stitched together and lined. You can decorate the bags with clusters of fabric roses, tassels, lace motifs or ribbon bows.

Most people generally have stray odds and ends that need tidying away in their home – earrings, necklaces, handkerchiefs, scarves, tiny keepsakes and sewing equipment such as embroidery floss, cotton reels and buttons. You could make several matching fabric bags as a gift and tie them up with huge ribbon bows so they can be left out on display rather than stored away in drawers.

▲ *These pretty bridesmaids' bags are made by gathering rectangles of taffeta on to a circular base. Matching fabric roses give them a suitably romantic appearance for a wedding celebration.*

Drawstring bag with a circular base

1 Cutting out Using the pair of compasses and pencil, draw a 13cm (5⅛in) diameter circle on to paper; or find a circular object of this size to draw around. Cut around the circle and use it as a pattern to cut two circles from fabric and one circle from interfacing. Cut two 40 x 28cm (15¾ x 11in) rectangles.

2 Marking the casing Lay out the two main fabric rectangles with wrong sides up. On both short sides of each rectangle, measure and mark 11.5cm (4½in) and 13cm (5⅛in) down from one long edge.

3 Stitching the sides Place the fabric rectangles right sides together. Stitch down one side seam to the first casing mark and backstitch. Start stitching again at the second casing mark, securing with backstitching, and stitch to the base edge. Repeat for the other side seam. Press the side seams open. Neaten the top raw edge by overlocking or stitching a double 6mm (¼in) hem.

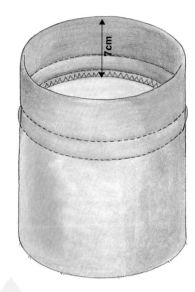

4 Making the casing Measure and mark 7cm (2¾in) from the top neatened edge and fold the fabric to the wrong side along this line. Press. Turn to the right side. To draw guidelines for the casing, use tailor's chalk to mark all the way round the bag in line with the top and bottom of the casing. Stitch along both lines.

▼ *For small scented decorations, make gathered bags in rich velvet, fill them with dried lavender or potpourri and close the neck with a tasseled cord. In the bags below, a Turk's head button nestles neatly in the center of each ruffle.*

You will need

- 30cm (⅜yd) of 112cm (44in) wide fabric
- 20cm (8in) of lightweight interfacing
- 1.2m (1½yd) of cord or ribbon
- Pair of compasses
- Pencil
- Sheet of paper
- Scissors
- Matching sewing thread
- Tailor's chalk
- Bodkin or small safety pin

5 Assembling the base Sandwich the interfacing circle between the two fabric circles, with the right sides of the fabric circles facing outwards. Tack around the edge of the circle.

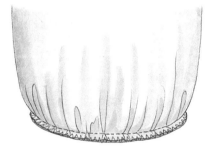

6 Attaching the base Work a row of gathering stitches around the bottom raw edge. With right sides together, pin the sides to the circular base, pulling up the gathers evenly to fit. Stitch the sides to the base. Neaten the seam allowances with a close zigzag stitch. Turn to the right side.

7 Adding the drawstring Cut two 60cm (24in) lengths of cord and thread them all the way round the casing in opposite directions. Thread on tassels. Knot the cords and adjust to hide the knots inside the casing.

Ribbon-embroidered cushions

*By using narrow ribbons instead of floss for
embroidery, you can create textured designs in next to no time,
like the beautiful floral wreath and bouquet here.*

Using a large-eyed needle, such as a chenille needle, you can stitch with double-sided ribbon and even work certain embroidery stitches to create all sorts of unusual effects. Very narrow ribbons are the most versatile because they can be twisted and turned into intricate shapes, but you can also work simple embroidery stitches with standard-width ribbons.

Ribbon covers more quickly than embroidery threads, and you will be

delighted to find how little time it takes to complete a project. Use lengths of about 20cm (8in) and cut the ribbon on a sharp diagonal to reduce fraying and to make threading the needle easier.

The thickness of the ribbon makes the stitching quite chunky, so you may wish to work any delicate or fine design lines with ordinary embroidery floss. Embroidery floss can also add greater textural interest. If you do this, always work the main ribbon areas first.

▲ *The designs on these romantic bed cushions were stitched with ribbons and then completed with some simple embroidery stitches using embroidery floss. The silk Dupion fabrics are the perfect complements for the satin ribbons and silky threads.*

Making the wreath cushion

This floral wreath is worked in narrow double-sided ribbons and pearl cotton thread using simple embroidery stitches.

For this project, the shape of the design makes it ideal for embellishing a circular cushion, but you could add it to a cushion cover of any shape or use it to decorate a scented sachet or other dainty fabric item. The peach and green color scheme of the ribbons can be varied to suit your own choice.

You will need

- 30cm (12in) circular cushion pad
- 2m (2¼yd) lace trim
- 50cm (⅝yd) silk Dupion
- Matching sewing thread
- 20cm (8in) embroidery hoop
- Number 18 chenille needle; embroidery needle
- 1m (1⅛yd) of 4mm (⅛in) wide light peachy pink silk ribbon
- 2m (2¼yd) of 4mm (⅛in) wide medium peachy pink silk ribbon
- 1.3m (1½yd) of 4mm (⅛in) wide dark peachy pink ribbon
- 1m (1⅛yd) of 4mm (⅛in) wide green silk ribbon
- Green (524) DMC number 8 pearl cotton
- Dressmaker's pencil
- Scissors and tape measure

1 Cutting out the fabric Cut two 33cm (13¼ in) circles of silk Dupion (the size of your cushion plus 1.5cm (⅝in) seam allowances all around).

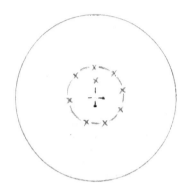

2 Marking the design Fold the fabric in half in each direction to find the center. Unfold the fabric and mark the center with crossed pins. Using the dressmaker's pencil, draw a circle 10.5cm (4⅛in) in diameter, centering on the pins. Mark the positions of the flowers.

3 Starting the flowers Mount the fabric in the frame so the design is centered. Use light peachy pink ribbon to work a single 1.5cm (⅝in) long bullion stitch for the center of each flower, wrapping the ribbon around the needle four times and keeping it flat.

4 Completing the flowers Using medium peachy pink ribbon, work a bullion stitch on each side of the first bullion. Change to dark peachy pink ribbon and work two or three straight stitches on each side of the flower to form the open petals, leaving spaces for leaves.

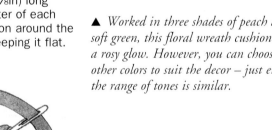

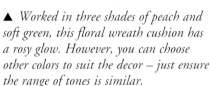

▲ *Worked in three shades of peach and soft green, this floral wreath cushion has a rosy glow. However, you can choose other colors to suit the decor – just ensure the range of tones is similar.*

5 Working buds and leaves Change back to the medium peachy pink ribbon to work straight stitches about 6mm (¼in) long for the flower buds. Use the green ribbon to work straight stitches the same size or longer for the leaves.

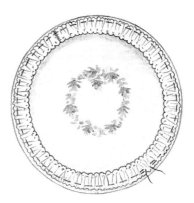

8 Attaching the lace Using the dressmaker's pencil, mark the stitching line on the embroidered circle, 1.5cm (⅝in) from the raw edge. Now work a row of gathering stitches 1cm (⅜in) from the unfinished edge of the lace. Pull up the gathers to fit the circle and pin and then tack to the stitching line with right sides facing.

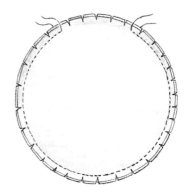

9 Attaching the back Pin the remaining circle of fabric on top of the embroidered circle with right sides facing and stitch all around, taking a 1.5cm (⅝in) seam allowance and leaving a gap of at least 20cm (8in) to insert the pad. Clip the seam allowances at regular intervals for ease, then turn right sides out.

6 Completing the embroidery Thread the embroidery needle with the green pearl cotton and work a fly stitch at the base of each bud. On some buds add an extra stitch in the center extending halfway up the bud, as shown. Join the flowers and buds with individual straight stitches.

7 Preparing the lace With right sides facing, join the ends of the lace together, taking a 1cm (⅜in) seam allowance. Make sure the lace isn't twisted. Trim the seam allowances by half and neaten them together with zigzag stitch.

10 Completing the cushion Tease the lace into a pleasing arrangement and insert the cushion pad. Tuck in the seam allowances at the opening and slipstitch it closed.

Making the bouquet cushion

This floral bouquet is quick and simple to embroider using double-sided ribbons in several widths and embroidery floss.

If you have trouble finding the specific ribbons or embroidery floss in your local stores, substitute something similar, or invent your own combination to suit a room scheme.

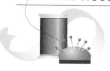
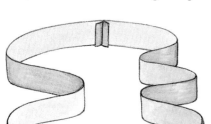

1 Cutting out fabric Cut two 33cm (13¼in) squares of silk Dupion (the size of your cushion plus 1.5cm (⅝in) seam allowances all around). Cut the remaining fabric into 10cm (4in) wide strips and join them together. Join the ends to make a loop.

2 Preparing the fabric Fold one fabric square in half in each direction to find the center. Unfold the fabric and mark the center with crossed pins. Mark a point 6cm (2⅜in) above the cross.

3 Working the first stitch Thread a 20cm (8in) length of peach ribbon and bring it up at the top mark. Work a vertical lazy daisy stitch about 2cm (¾in) long.

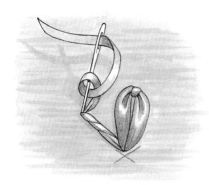

4 Working the stamens Bring the needle back up at the mark and twist the needle around and around until the ribbon forms a tube. Take the needle back into fabric at the tip of the stamen, about 2cm (¾in) away. Work a single-wrap French knot at the top. Work three more stamens so there are two on each side of the center petal.

5 Completing the flower Using apricot ribbon, work three straight stitches around the flower, sometimes twisting the ribbon for natural variation. Change to organza ribbon and work two more petals in the same way. Finally, work the sepals at the base of the flower in straight stitch with green ribbon.

6 Working the remaining flowers Work the remaining four flowers in the same way. Then stitch the stems in stem stitch using two strands of embroidery floss and finishing at the crossed pins. Work the leaves over the stems with the green ribbon, making short, straight stitches. Remove the crossed pins.

7 Adding the bow Make a bow in the variegated ribbon by crossing it over itself and stitching the bow 'knot' to the fabric at the bottom of the embroidered stems. Secure the ribbon by working evenly spaced French knots in two strands of peach or cream thread to match the ribbon.

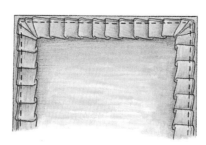

8 Adding the frill Fold the long fabric strip in half lengthways and pleat it at about 2.5cm (1in) intervals. Pin the pleats along the raw edges, then tack the strip to the embroidered square with raw edges matching, adjusting the pleats as necessary for a good fit.

9 Completing the cushion Lay the remaining fabric square on top with right sides facing and stitch together, taking a 1.5cm (⅝in) seam allowance and leaving a gap in one edge. Trim the seam allowance at corners and turn right sides out. Insert the cushion pad and slipstitch the gap closed.

▲ *This stunning design uses unusual organza and variegated ribbons to make it extra special, but you may wish to substitute other attractive ribbons you find locally.*

Creative couching

With couching you can add sparkle, texture and glamour to
your work using metal threads, ornate cords and other threads
too thick or too delicate to be stitched through the fabric.

Couching is the simple technique of attaching decorative threads or cords to fabric by oversewing them with tiny stitches in a matching thread. The technique dates back thousands of years, and was particularly popular as a means of adorning the court clothes of royalty and aristocrats. Today it is used for ecclesiastical vestments and altar frontals and for military uniforms, but you can use it to adorn evening dresses, small furnishings, wall hangings and pictures – whatever would benefit from a little sparkle.

Threads

Japanese gold/silver is a flat strip of 'gold' or 'silver' coiled around core threads. It comes in several thicknesses from 1K (thick) to 4K (thin). The 1K version is used for the frame shown in the picture.

Twists are metal threads that are twisted together. They tarnish slightly over time, so ask your supplier for information on the best types to use.

Lurex is made of synthetic material and doesn't tarnish.

Purls are metal wires tightly coiled to

▲ *This gorgeous picture frame is decorated in gold threads. The thicker thread is couched in place while the thinner one is worked in lines of backstitch. Together these stitches recreate the look of land contours on a map.*

create a beaded effect. They can be couched in long lengths or cut into short lengths and stitched to the fabric like beads.

Plate is a flat strip of metal, generally couched in a zigzag pattern.

Making the frame

The embroidery on this frame is based on the contours of a map, making it particularly suitable for framing landscape photos. However, as you can see from the picture on the previous page, it works well with any type of image. Use silver or gold threads, according to preference.

You will need

- ◆ **Photo frame with a flat molding**
- ◆ **Card cut to fit the frame**
- ◆ **Lightweight batting cut to fit the frame**
- ◆ **Tracing paper**
- ◆ **Rectangle of silk or other fabric 5cm (2in) larger all round than the frame**
- ◆ **Cotton fabric for backing to fit the embroidery frame**
- ◆ **Slate frame**
- ◆ **1K Japanese gold or other thick metal thread**
- ◆ **Matching sewing thread**
- ◆ **Thin metal thread or embroidery floss**
- ◆ **Small embroidery needle; large chenille needle and a sewing needle**
- ◆ **Map with land contours**
- ◆ **Pens in two colors**
- ◆ **Strong multi-purpose glue**
- ◆ **Tweezers**

▶ *Worked in gold threads on a bronze-tinted background, the embroidered frame has a stately look, but you could choose any combination you like, such as silver, blue or bronze on red-brown or black fabric.*

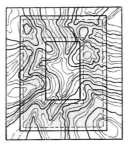

1 Preparing the design Choose a suitable part of the map with attractive contours. Enlarge this area of the map on a photocopier until the land contours are sufficiently wide apart. You may need to experiment with different sections and enlargements to get a good design for your frame. Mark the size of your frame and its aperture on the map, adding 1cm (⅜in) in each direction to allow for the padding and to provide an overlap. Darken the frame outline so it stands out clearly.

3 Preparing the fabric Hem the sides of the backing fabric for strength and mount in the slate frame. Tack the embroidery fabric on top and then tack the tracing over this through both fabric layers.

2 Completing the pattern Tape tracing paper over the photocopy and mark the frame area. Mark in the main land contours with one pen and the other land contours in another color. Smooth out contour lines if necessary for the most attractive design. Discard the photocopy.

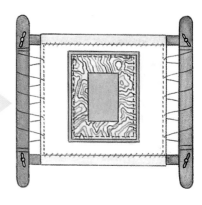

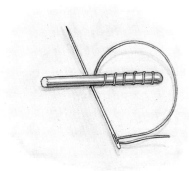

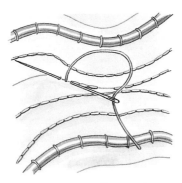

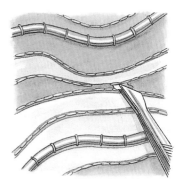

4 Couching the main contours Work the design in sections to make it easier to remove the tracing paper afterwards. Stitching through the tracing paper, couch the thick gold thread to the principal contours of one area (see *Stitch library* below). Take the ends of the couching thread to the back of the work and secure them as you go. Do not leave this until the end.

5 Working the smaller contours Using the thin metal thread in the embroidery needle, work the remaining contours in backstitch. In places where the lines are very close together, you can 'feather' them by dropping the second or third line and then starting it again where the space widens.

6 Removing the tracing Remove the tracing paper as you complete each section. To do this, use the point of a needle to score along the tracing close to each stitching line. Pull out the tracing paper strips with tweezers, using the sharp points to remove tiny bits stuck under the stitching. Gently does it. Complete the embroidery in the same way.

Stitch library

Couching

This is a simple technique which enables you to use thick or delicate threads in embroidery designs.

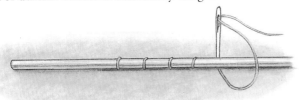

1 Getting started Lay the decorative thread on the line to be stitched, leaving a short end which can be taken to the back of the work later. Thread a sewing needle with fine matching thread and bring it up just past the starting point. Take it over the decorative thread and back into the fabric close to where it emerged.

2 Working the line Work the same stitch at 6mm (¼in) intervals along the decorative thread. To finish, slip a chenille needle into the fabric at each end, slide the decorative thread through the eye and pass it to the back of the fabric. Work a few stitches over the thread on the back of the fabric to secure it.

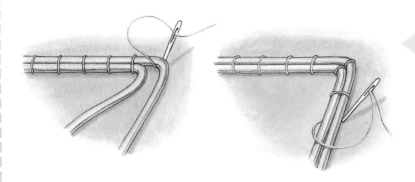

3 Working with two threads Metal threads are often couched in pairs. Couch the threads as one except at corners when you should couch the outer thread first, then the inner thread and then continue as before.

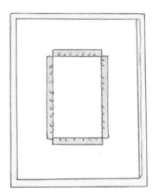

7 **Preparing the card** Measure and mark a rectangle the size of the frame, marking the size and position of the aperture at the same time. Cut this out and check it against the picture frame for fit. Glue the batting to the card and leave to dry. Then trim it to match the card around the outer edges and aperture.

8 **Preparing the fabric** Remove the embroidery from the frame. Trim the embroidery fabric and backing 2cm (¾in) larger than the embroidered area; at internal corners trim the embroidered fabric diagonally almost to the stitching and add a dab of glue to prevent fraying. Turn the work over and trim the backing close to the stitching.

9 **Gluing the inner edges** Lay out the embroidery right side down and center the card, batting side down, on top. Apply a thin line of glue to the edges of the fabric around the card aperture and spread it with a strip of card or a glue spatula. Allow to dry. Apply a line of glue to the inner edge of the card, then bring the fabric edges over and press in place. The edges of the embroidery should be just visible on the folds. If you need to adjust the fabric's position, do so while the glue is still wet.

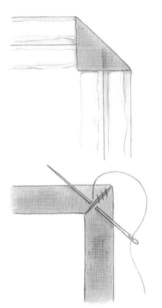

10 **Gluing the outer edges** Apply glue to the fabric edges around the outside of the frame and leave to dry. Now apply glue to the corresponding card edges. Glue the corners of the fabric in place first, folding them over diagonally as shown. Then fold in the remaining raw edges and press under a clean sheet of paper and a few books for an hour or so while the glue dries. Oversew the folded fabric at the corners as shown.

11 **Finishing the frame** Apply glue evenly to the inner and outer edges of the photo frame, spreading it with card or a spatula. Place the embroidered frame on top and press it down firmly with your fingers. Lay a sheet of clean paper over the top and leave the work to dry overnight under books or other weights.

▶ *Silk and metallic threads are the raw materials of the couching technique that brings a courtly glamour to clothes and interior design.*

Fabric roses

Romantic full-blown roses, formed from layers of fabric petals, may be used to embellish gift boxes and they also make delightful gifts in their own right.

These beautiful full-blown fabric roses resemble the extravagant, old-fashioned cabbage roses so loved by traditional plant enthusiasts. The soft blooms look professional, yet they are surprisingly simple to make. Even if you lack sewing experience, the easy folding and stitching method will guarantee good results.

The roses can be applied singly or in clusters to all sorts of items, from gift boxes and plush photograph frames, to cushions, a hat or the edge of a tablecloth. They look charming clustered on a tieback or dotted singly at the base of goblet pleats on a curtain. A few small blooms could even be pinned at the waist of a dress for a special occasion.

Almost any fabric is suitable, depending on the look you want to achieve, but avoid heavy or stiff fabrics which are difficult to shape and stitch. For a rich look, make the roses in velvet, choosing deep colors such as crimson or dusty

▲ *A cluster of full-blown roses in a medley of pink and gold silks and taffetas forms a harmonious picture on the lid of an old gold box, and gives a hint of delectable treasures hidden within.*

pink. Satin gives the petals a realistic sheen, while roses made from filmy muslin have a fragile quality. Natural cotton roses in bright clear colors add a splash of informality to a room.

Making full-blown roses

The roses are made by folding fabric squares into triangles, which are then stitched together into a square – this forms one petal layer. These steps explain how to make a rose with three layers of petals and a separate center. To make smaller roses, either cut smaller fabric squares in step **1**, or use a rose center with just one or two petal layers. You should be able to make several full-size blooms from a 50cm (20in) length of fabric. You will also need matching sewing thread, a sewing needle and pins.

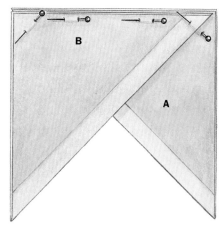

1 Cutting out *For the petal layers:* on the straight grain, cut four 12.5cm (5in) squares, four 10cm (4in) squares and four 7.5cm (3in) squares. *For the rose center:* on the bias, cut a 12.5 x 5cm (5 x 2in) strip. *For the back of the rose:* cut a circle of fabric 6.5cm (2½in) in diameter.

2 Preparing the pieces Wrong sides together, fold each square in half diagonally, to form a triangle; press. Wrong sides together, press bias strip in half lengthways. Then, along all the folded edges, fold a further 6mm (¼in) to the back; finger press the narrow folds or press lightly with an iron, then open them out.

▼ *A red satin rose looks sumptuous on a napkin ring. To make the leaves, place batting between two pieces of fabric, then machine satin stitch a leaf shape through all the layers; trim close to stitching. Try making roses in a range of sizes. The small blooms (right) have just one petal layer.*

3 Starting outer petals Using the 12.5cm (5in) squares, and calling them **A-D**, start making the outer petals. Lay triangle **A** flat, with back uppermost and pin triangle **B** on top, with folded edges crossing at right angles and raw edges matching.

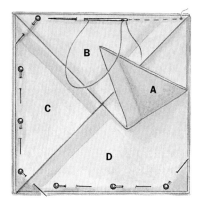

4 Finishing the outer petals Overlap and pin the remaining triangles **C** and **D** in the same way to form a square, overlapping the previous triangle at one side each time. Lift the corner of **A** to tuck the corner of **D** to the back. Work a row of gathering stitches along one side of the square.

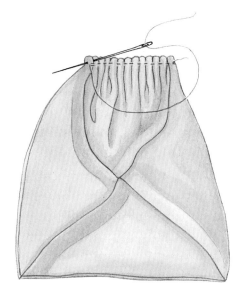

5 Gathering up the petals Pull up the gathering stitches tightly and secure them with small backstitches. Repeat along the remaining sides of the square, so the folded edges turn outwards to form one layer of petals. Finger press narrow folds to the back.

6 Making the inner petal layers Follow steps **3-5** to make up two more layers of petals, this time using the 10cm (4in) and 7.5cm (3in) squares respectively.

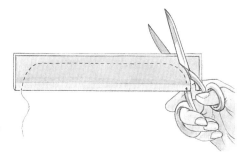

7 Making rose center Work a row of gathering stitches along the raw edges of the folded bias strip, curving towards the folded edge at each end. Trim around the curve at the corners. Pull up the stitches until the strip is half original length. Then wrap the strip around itself and finger press a narrow fold to the outside. Stitch securely at base.

8 Arranging the layers Place the rose center inside the smallest petal layer. Stitch them together, so that the stitches are not visible from top of the rose. Arrange larger petal layers around them; stitch together, one layer at a time. To finish, slipstitch the circle of fabric to back of rose, tucking raw edges under as you work. Stitch roses in place on chosen item.

Travelling companions

A softly padded jewelry roll and make-up bag, made from sumptuous silks and satins, will allow the bride to keep her baubles and cosmetics safe when travelling on honeymoon.

Such a cleverly designed jewelry roll could be said to be worth its weight in gold! Made in blue and pink satin, with piped edges, it has three separate inside pockets – each one the width of the roll – with neat zipper closures to ensure that favorite brooches, bracelets, earrings and other items of jewelry are completely safe while being carried around.

A handy ring holder is attached to the front of the middle pocket. This small padded roll is secured at one end with a strong press stud – you simply unfasten it when you want to slip rings on or off. When the jewelry roll is closed, the rings are held safely in the center. There is also a pocket for larger items, such as necklaces, concealed within the lining.

Made from pure silks, the make-up bag is lined and lightly padded. The contrast flap is piped around the edge and the bag is tied in a pretty double bow, using 1/8 grosgrain ribbon.

The jewelry roll is compact, yet large enough to hold vacation jewelry. The padding protects delicate pieces from damage, and the soft shape ensures that it will tuck into a corner of an overnight bag. Stitch a make-up bag to match – perfect for travelling.

Making the jewelry roll

Suitable fabrics for the jewelry roll include light to mediumweight silks, satins, brocades, damasks and cottons in either bright or subtle colors. For the decorative piped edging, which gives support to the seams, buy ready-made covered piping. This comes in a wide range of colors.

The finished jewelry roll measures about 29 x 20cm (11½ x 8in). Take 1.2cm (½in) seam allowances throughout, unless otherwise stated.

You will need

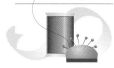

- 30cm (¼yd) of fabric for the outside and pockets
- 30cm (¼yd) of contrast fabric for the inner lining
- 40 x 23cm (16 x 9in) of 50g (2oz) batting
- 1m (1⅛yd) of ready-made covered piping
- 1m (1⅛yd) of 3mm (⅛in) wide ribbon
- Three nylon zippers, 20cm (8in) long, to match the contrast lining
- One clear snap fastener
- Embroidery floss in contrast color
- Crewel needle, size 9
- Bodkin

Tip

BULKY ZIPPERS
Before you start stitching round the jewelry roll in step 9, move the zipper pulls away from the edge, to make the machine stitching easier.

1 Cutting out *From main fabric:* cut one 32 x 23cm (12½ x 9in) rectangle for the back, and one 20 x 6cm (8 x 2¼in) rectangle for the ring roll; cut three 23 x 10cm (9 x 4in) pieces and one 23 x 6cm (9 x 2½in) piece for the pockets. *From contrast fabric:* cut two 32 x 23cm (12½ x 9in) rectangles for the pocket linings.

2 Applying the batting Cut a 23 x 8cm (9 x 3½in) strip from one edge of the batting for the ring roll and put to one side. Place the remaining batting on the wrong side of the back rectangle, raw edges even. Pin and tack the two layers together across the center both ways and 2.5cm (1in) in from the outside edge.

3 Working the French knots Thread the crewel needle with three strands of embroidery floss and work groups of three French knots at random over the surface, to hold the batting in place. Avoid working into the seam allowance. Trim the batting so that it is 1.2cm (½in) smaller all around than the fabric.

4 Piping the edge With raw edges matching, pin the piping around the right side of the back section, beginning and ending at center of one long side and overlapping ends. Tack in place. Cut two ribbon ties 33cm (13in) long; with raw edges even, tack to center top. Machine stitch all around.

5 Making the ring roll Fold ring roll fabric in half lengthways, right sides together. Taking a 6mm (¼in) seam, stitch the long side. Turn to the right side. Roll the reserved batting tightly and, with a threaded bodkin, pull it through the fabric tube. Trim the tube to 18cm (7in), turn in the raw fabric edges and slipstitch to hold.

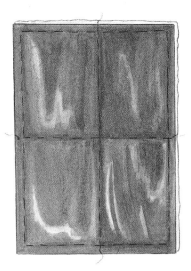

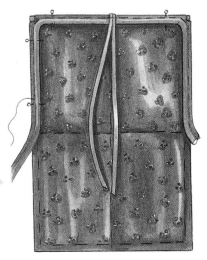

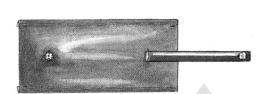

6 Attaching the ring roll Turn under seam allowances on long sides of all main fabric pocket pieces; press. Pin one end of ring roll to a larger pocket piece. Pin and stitch 6mm (¼in) from end. Attach half snap fastener to ring roll and other half to pocket piece.

7 Starting the pockets Pin, tack and stitch a zipper to top edge of another large pocket piece, stitching 6mm (¼in) from the edge. Pin and tack other edge of zipper to lower edge of ring roll pocket. Pin pockets and zipper right side up on to one pocket lining, with lower raw edges matching. Stitching through *all* layers, stitch *top* edge of zipper.

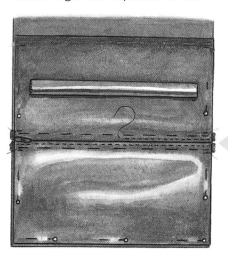

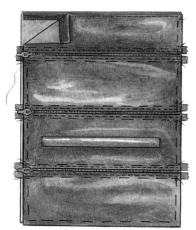

8 Completing the pockets Repeat step **7** to attach the remaining pockets, placing the small pocket piece at the top. Tack through all layers along the long sides and the base edge. On the top edge, trim the pocket lining to size. Turn the seam allowances to the wrong side, and topstitch through all layers.

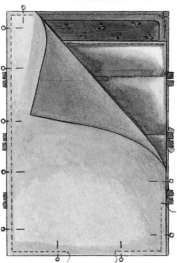

9 Assembling layers Lay back piece right side up. Place zipped pocket section, then second pocket lining, both right side down, on top of back piece. Align lower and side edges, then pin and stitch all around, leaving an 11cm (4½in) opening on lower edge.

▲ *When the roll is open, there is access to three small pockets, one large pocket and a padded roll for securing rings.*

10 Turning through Trim the corners and seam allowances. Turn through so that the back and pocket linings are on the outside. Working inside opening, stitch back and pocket lining together. Turn in pocket lining seam allowances and machine stitch across to neaten. Turn to right side.

11 Finishing off Cut the remaining ribbon into 10cm (4in) lengths; knot into the ends of the zipper pulls.

Make-up bag

Except for the batting, all of the fabric measurements include a 1.2cm (½in) seam allowance. The finished make-up bag measures 19 x 15cm (7½ x 6in).

You will need

- 37 x 26cm (14½ x 10in) fabric for the outer bag
- 22 x 12cm (8½ x 4½in) contrast fabric for the flap
- 47 x 26cm (18½ x 10in) of lining fabric
- 47 x 26cm (18½ x 10in) of 50g (2oz) batting
- 70cm (27in) of ready-made covered piping
- Four 25cm (10in) lengths of 3mm (⅛in) wide ribbon
- Paper, ruler and pencil

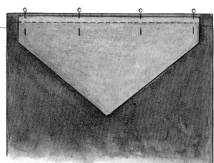

1 Making the flap pattern On paper, measure and draw a 22 x 12cm (8½ x 4½in) rectangle. At each side, mark 2.5cm (1in) up from the bottom edge, and mark the center top edge. Using a ruler, join the points. Cut out.

2 Attaching the flap Pin the pattern for the flap on to the contrast fabric and cut out. With right sides together, pin the flap to the outer bag rectangle, centering the flap on one short side. Stitch. Press seam open.

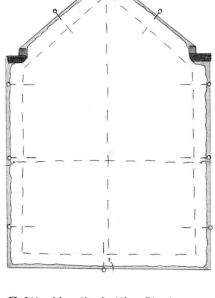

3 Attaching the batting Pin the batting to the wrong side of the bag. Trim the batting to shape, trimming off the seam allowances, and then tack it to the bag.

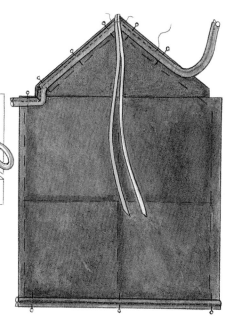

4 Applying the piping On the right side of the bag, pin and tack the piping around the flap and along the bottom edge. Tack two of the 25cm (10in) long ribbon ties to the flap point, matching the raw edges. Stitch the piping in place.

5 Side seams Open out the flap; then, with right sides together, fold the bag in half. Pin, tack and then stitch the side seams. Press the seams open.

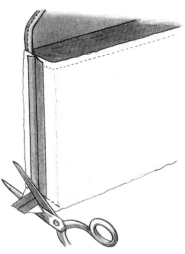

6 Making the gusset Working on the wrong side, flatten the bottom corners of the bag to a width of 4cm (1½in). Pin and stitch. Trim across, and turn the bag to the right side.

7 Attaching the front ties Mark the position for the ties 9cm (3½in) down from the center of the top edge. Stitch the ties firmly in place, turning under the ends to neaten.

8 Making the lining Trim the seam allowance off the lower edge of the flap pattern. Center the pattern at the top of the lining rectangle; pin, and then cut around it. Stitch the side seams and make the gusset in the same way as the main fabric bag. Leave wrong side out.

9 Attaching the lining Slip the lining inside the bag, with right sides together. Pin and stitch together around the flap and top edge, leaving a gap to turn through. Trim seams and snip into the corners; then turn through to the right side. Slip the lining inside the bag. Turn in the seam allowance along the gap and slipstitch it closed.

10 Defining the gusset Make a tiny pleat at the top edge of the bag at each side seam and secure with one or two stitches.

Traditional teddies

These adorable teddy bears – each one with an endearing character all its own – will delight dedicated collectors and newly converted bear lovers alike.

Teddy bears are universally loved by both young and old, and these traditional-style teddies, with their jointed necks, arms and legs, are irresistible. The different fabrics give individual character and each has its own unique expression. The teddies are intended for older bear lovers, and not as playthings for young children.

There is a wide range of fabrics to choose from. If you like, splash out on an extravagant fur fabric – even the larger bear takes only 25cm (⅜yd) of main fabric. Mohair is one of many luxury options – you can choose from a range of finishes, from thick, soft piles to long, wild and eccentric.

For a more economical teddy, use a synthetic fur, or give an old fun-fur coat a new lease of life – keep an eye on your local consignment stores for interesting finds.

▲ *Don't assume that a teddy must be brown and furry; many other soft fabrics, such as richly colored crushed velvet, will make lovable bears with their own endearing natures.*

There are two sizes of teddy to choose from – the larger one is 30cm (12in) tall, and the smaller one is 24cm (9½in) tall.

Making a teddy bear

Plastic animal joints and safety eyes are fixed before the bear is stuffed. Glass eyes (never use these for a child's toy) are added after stuffing. All are available from needlecraft departments and suppliers of toy-making equipment. To stuff the bears, polyester toy filling is ideal; or use plastic pellets for a different feel.

All the pattern pieces include a 6mm (¼in) seam allowance. When cutting out, use the point of the scissors and cut through the backing fabric only, and not the fur. Always pin the fabric pieces together before stitching to prevent slipping, and clip all seam allowances before turning to right side.

You will need

For a large teddy:

- 25cm (³⁄₈yd) fur fabric
- Three sets of 35mm (1½in) joints for neck and arms
- Two sets of 45mm (1¾in) joints for legs
- Two 8mm (¼in) wide plastic safety or glass eyes

For a small teddy:

- 76 x 36cm (30 x 14in) fur fabric
- Five sets 30mm (1¼in) joints for neck, arms, legs
- Two 7mm (¼in) wide plastic safety or glass eyes

For both size bears:

- Scraps of felt or suedette for paws and feet
- Tracing paper and pencil
- Dressmaker's pencil
- Sewing thread to match fur fabric
- Black or brown pearl embroidery floss
- Polyester toy filling or plastic pellets
- Button thread and long needle (optional)

1 Making a pattern Trace all the pattern pieces for the appropriate size of bear on to tracing paper, including the joint positions and opening marks. Cut out the traced pattern pieces.

2 Cutting out Lay the fabric in a single layer fur side down with the pile downwards. Position pattern pieces with the arrows pointing in the direction of the fur pile and pin in place. Cut out the required number of each piece, reversing the pattern as indicated. Mark all joint positions with a dressmaker's pencil. Cut foot pads and paws from felt or suedette.

3 Stitching the ears Pin two ear pieces right sides together, and stitch, leaving an opening between markings. Trim corners, clip curves, and turn right side out. Turn in the open edges and oversew. Repeat for the second ear.

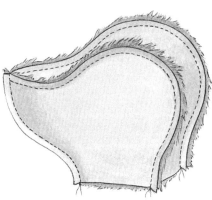

4 Stitching the head Pin the side head pieces right sides together and stitch the chin seam. Right sides together, pin the head gusset in place, matching the chin seam to the center of the nose. Stitch along one side from nose to neck opening, then stitch the other side from nose to neck. Clip the seam allowances.

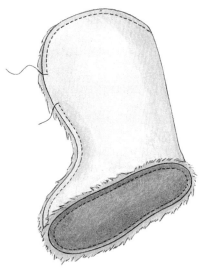

5 Stitching the legs With right sides together, fold the legs in half and pin. Stitch, leaving an opening between markings. Clip into seam allowances. With right sides together, pin the foot pads in position, matching the front and back points. Tack firmly to prevent them slipping. Stitch and clip the seam allowances.

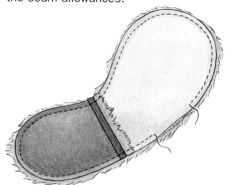

6 Stitching the arms With right sides together, and matching straight edges, pin and stitch felt paws to inner arms. Pin and stitch inner arms to outer arms, leaving an opening between the markings.

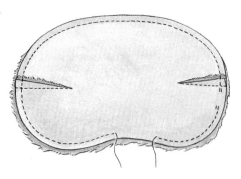

7 Stitching the body With right sides together, pin and stitch top and bottom darts. Pin body pieces right sides together and stitch, leaving an opening between the markings on the back seam and a gap for neck joint.

With a wide range of fur fabric to choose from, each teddy bear takes on his own unique character. Plastic safety joints, shown here, make easy work of assembling the bears.

Filling and jointing the teddy

1 Fixing safety eyes If using safety eyes, turn the head to right side and stuff with polyester toy filling. Mark position of eyes with pins, make a small hole at each position and insert eye stalks through the holes from the right side. Take out stuffing and push the locking discs firmly on to the eye stalks from the back.

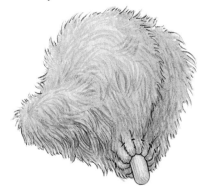

2 Inserting the neck joint Fill the head firmly with polyester toy filling. Using button thread, gather the neck edge and insert the neck joint so that the stalk protrudes from the base of the head. Pull the gathering thread tight and secure ends firmly.

3 Jointing the legs and arms Make small holes at the marked joint positions on legs and arms and turn through to the right side. Insert the stalk of the joint through the holes from inside the limbs, push them through the corresponding hole in the body and fix each in place inside the body with disc and locking washer.

4 Attaching the head to the body Push the stalk of the neck joint through the hole at the top of the body. Lock it in place inside the body as before.

5 Filling the arms, legs and body Fill arms and legs and then the body with polyester toy filling or plastic pellets, inserting it through the openings in the seams. Use a knitting needle to push the stuffing firmly into the ends of the paws and feet. Slipstitch the openings in leg, arm and back body seams.

Finishing the teddy bear

1 **Attaching the ears** Pin the ears in place firmly. Stitch, starting at the inner corner and working down.

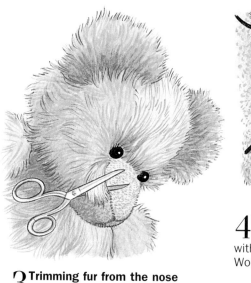

3 **Trimming fur from the nose** Using sharp scissors, trim the pile of the fur close to the backing fabric around the nose.

4 **Embroidering the face** Choose a shape of nose and embroider it with satin stitch using pearl cotton. Work mouth with two straight stitches.

2 **Attaching glass eyes** If using glass eyes, position the eyes and make small holes. Thread a long needle with button thread; insert from the back of the head through to one eye hole, leaving a thread end. Run the thread through the eye shank and insert the needle back through eye hole and out at the back of the head. Pull tight and tie the two thread ends together. Thread both ends on to the needle and stitch back inside the head. Repeat for second eye.

▶ *Trimming the fur from the nose helps to enhance each bear's loveable expression. The positioning of the eyes and stitching of nose and mouth make each face unique. A ribbon bow is all that is needed by way of adornment.*

Full-size traceable patterns for teddy bears

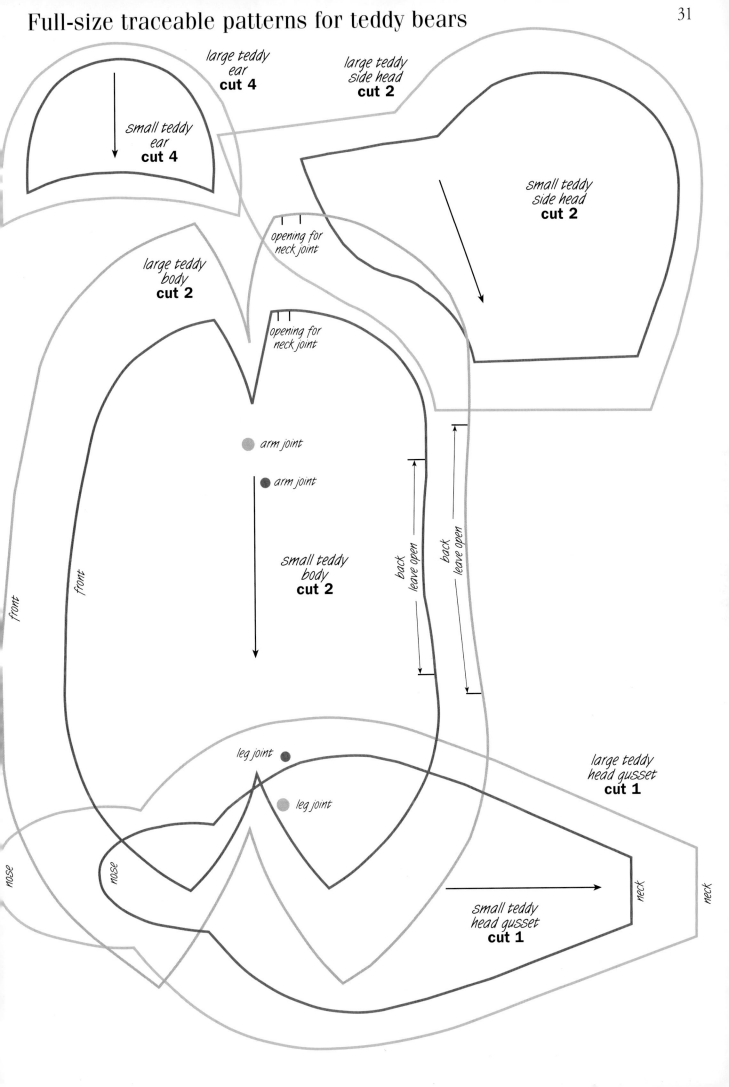

large teddy ear **cut 4**

small teddy ear **cut 4**

large teddy side head **cut 2**

small teddy side head **cut 2**

opening for neck joint

large teddy body **cut 2**

opening for neck joint

arm joint

arm joint

small teddy body **cut 2**

back leave open

back leave open

front

front

leg joint

leg joint

large teddy head gusset **cut 1**

nose

nose

small teddy head gusset **cut 1**

neck

neck

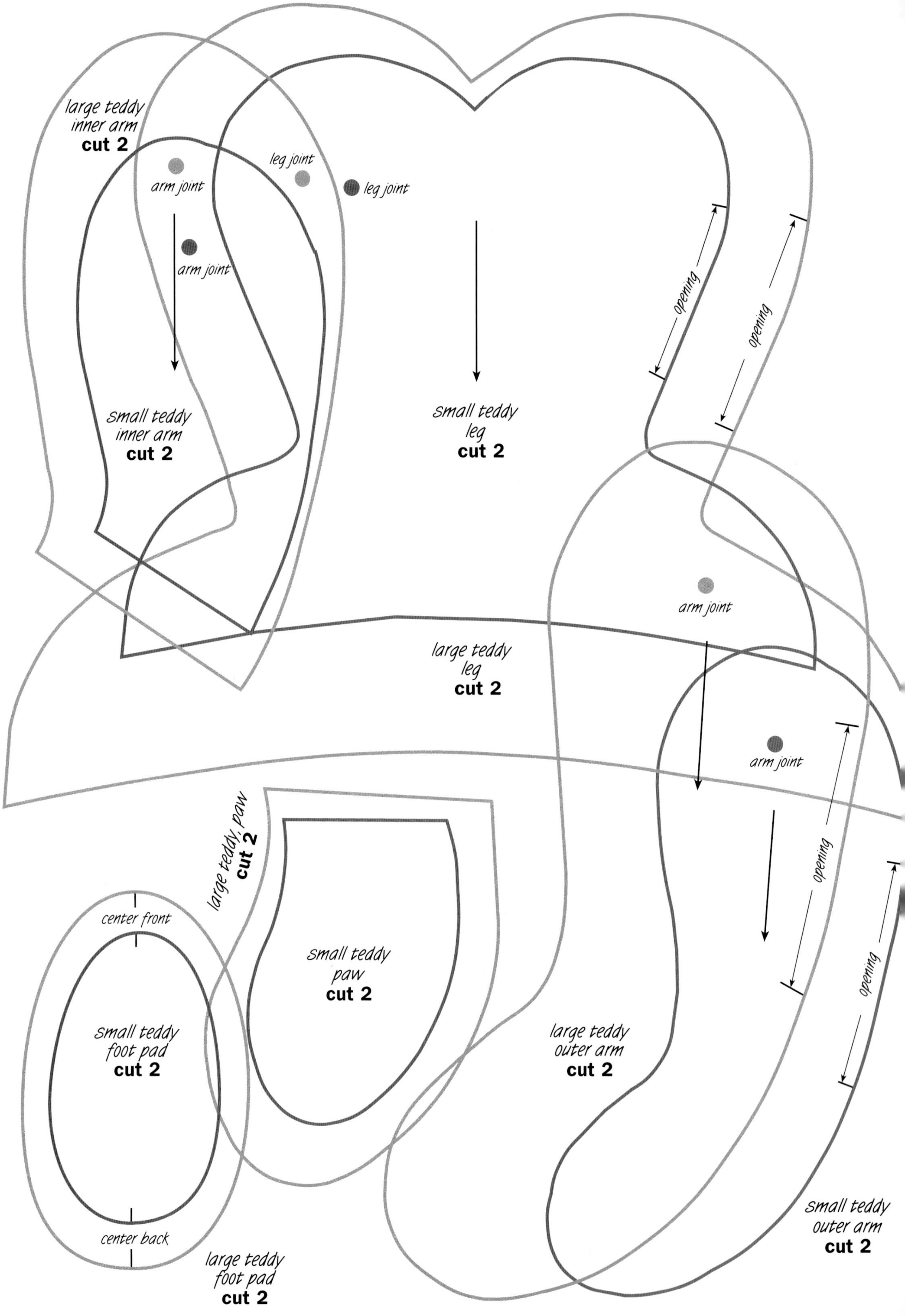

large teddy
inner arm
cut 2

arm joint

leg joint

leg joint

arm joint

small teddy
inner arm
cut 2

small teddy
leg
cut 2

opening

opening

arm joint

large teddy
leg
cut 2

arm joint

opening

opening

large teddy, paw
cut 2

center front

small teddy
paw
cut 2

small teddy
foot pad
cut 2

large teddy
outer arm
cut 2

center back

large teddy
foot pad
cut 2

small teddy
outer arm
cut 2

Rag dolls

Cuddly rag dolls are firm childhood favorites, and these two enchanting characters, with their colorful outfits and individual hairstyles, will delight children of all ages.

The appeal of rag dolls never fades and many generations of children have numbered them among their favorite toys. These two delightful characters, with their wide-eyed expressions and pretty clothes, are irresistible and will go straight to the hearts of their lucky recipients.

The finished dolls are approximately 50cm (20in) tall – plenty big enough for a good cuddle. Their outfits are easy to put on and take off, even for a young child. Both dolls and their outfits are made from the same patterns, but by changing the fabric color and hairstyles and dressing them in different clothes,

▲ *These charming dolls are made from one basic pattern – the choice of fabrics and hair styling gives each one individuality.*

they take on quite distinct characters. Instructions for making the dolls are given overleaf; steps for making the dolls' clothes are on pages 37–40.

Making the rag dolls

All the pattern pieces include 1cm (⅜in) seam allowances. Stitch the seams with right sides together and the raw edges matching, unless otherwise stated, and match centers, marks and dots. Snip into curves and across corners and press seams open unless otherwise stated.

For the doll's body, use any closely woven plain fabric, such as calico or a lightweight polyester/cotton. The boots are cut from black glazed cotton.

The mouth, nose and freckles are painted on with fabric paints. For the mouth and nose, choose a pink that will stand out well against the fabric; for the freckles, choose a color a few shades darker than the main fabric.

You will need

For both dolls:

- 50cm (⅝yd) of 90cm (36in) wide fabric for the body
- 20cm (¼yd) of black glazed cotton fabric for the boots
- 50cm (⅝yd) of 1.5cm (⅝in) wide satin ribbon for the hair
- Washable polyester toy filling
- Two black 1cm (⅜in) diameter toy safety eyes
- Six small black buttons with shanks
- Fine paint brush
- Fabric paints
- Matching sewing threads
- Tracing paper and pencil
- Dressmaker's pencil
- Knitting needle

For the long-haired doll:

- Mohair wool

For the curly-haired doll:

- 30cm (⅜yd) of lightweight cotton fabric

1 Cutting out Trace the pattern pieces given on page 36, including pattern markings, on to tracing paper and cut out. Lay pattern pieces on to fabric and cut them out, making sure you cut the right number of each. Transfer all pattern markings to fabric pieces with a dressmaker's pencil. Transfer the face to front head only.

2 Painting the face Using the paint brush and fabric paints, paint the mouth, nose and freckles on to right side of front head piece. Fix paints following manufacturer's instructions. Fix the safety eyes in position, as on page 42 step **4**.

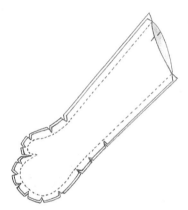

5 Stitching the arms Stitch the arms together in pairs, stitching through the dot at the thumb and leaving the straight ends open. Snip up to the dot and into the curves. Turn to the right side and pad firmly, pushing the filling into the thumb with a knitting needle. Tack across the straight ends.

8 Finishing the legs Fold each leg and boot in half, right sides together, and stitch down back seam. Tack, then stitch a boot sole to each foot. Turn out and pad with filling, then tack across the top, matching center dots to back seams. Sew three buttons to the outer sides of boots at marked positions.

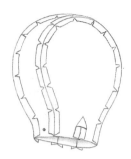

3 Stitching the head Stitch the head darts, then snip across corner of darts and press open. Place the head gusset between the two head pieces, matching marks; stitch. Snip the seam allowances at the curves and press open. Turn right side out.

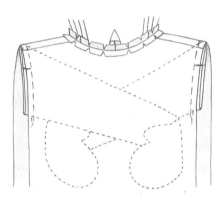

6 Attaching arms to body Tack the arms to the right side of one body piece, with the thumbs pointing upwards and the marks matching.

9 Joining the legs and body Matching dots and with the feet facing forwards, stitch the legs to the lower edge of the front body. Stitch the body side seams, with the arms tucked inside. Turn out and pad the head and body. Turn under 1cm (⅜in) on the lower edge of the back body and slipstitch in place.

4 Joining head and body pieces Stitch the body pieces together at the shoulders. With right sides together, pin the head to the body at the neck edges, matching the gusset dots to the shoulder seams; handsew neatly in place.

7 Stitching the legs Stitch the boot uppers together in pairs along the front seams. Open them out flat. Then, matching marks, stitch one boot upper to the lower edge of each leg. Press the seams towards the boots.

Adding the hair

Stitching long hair For the fringe, cut 10cm (4in) lengths of wool; fold in half in pairs. Backstitch in place along front gusset seam for 3cm (1¼in) on each side of top center. Repeat to stitch 60cm (24in) lengths along the marked hairlines on gusset and back head. Tie the hair in a pony tail at top of head.

Stitching short hair Tear lightweight cotton into 10 x 2cm (4 x ¾in) strips. Tie a knot in center of each. With matching thread, stitch knots over head gusset and back head.

▲ *The dolls' heads have a gusset at the side which adds more realistic depth and gives them a fuller head of hair. You can make the hair as wild and as colorful as you like; for a finishing touch, tie it up with a brightly colored ribbon bow.*

Full-size traceable patterns

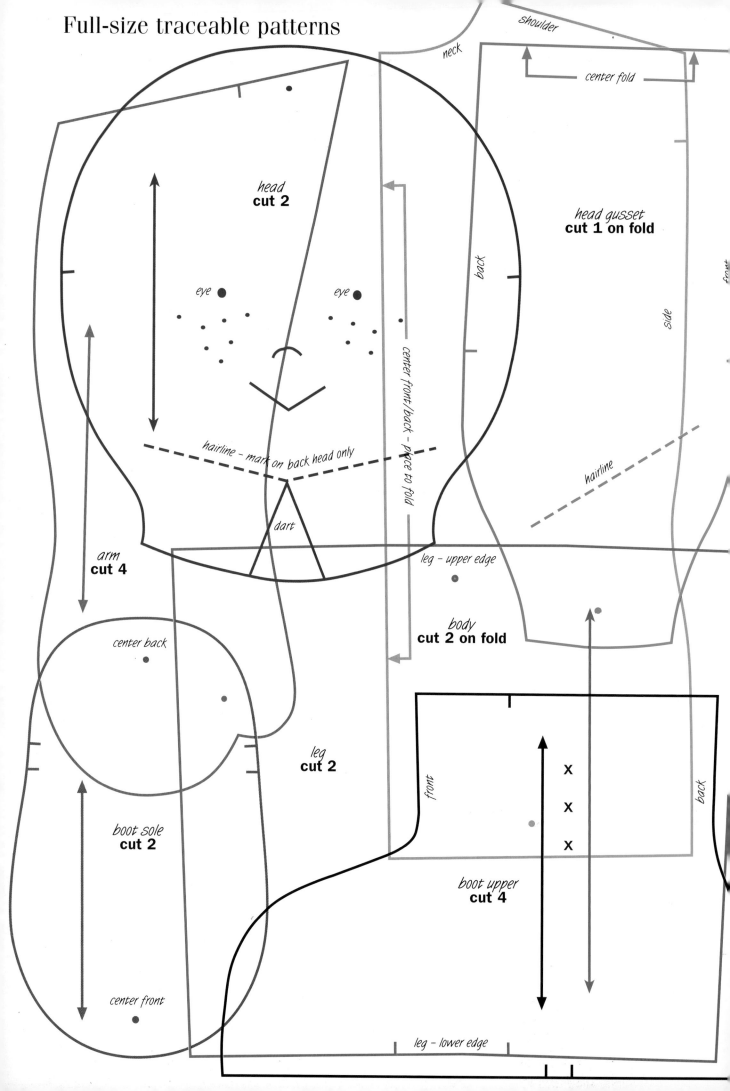

head
cut 2

eye ●   eye ●

hairline – mark on back head only

dart

arm
cut 4

center back

boot sole
cut 2

center front

leg
cut 2

neck

shoulder

center fold

head gusset
cut 1 on fold

back

side

hairline

center front/back – place to fold

leg – upper edge

body
cut 2 on fold

front

back

x
x
x

boot upper
cut 4

leg – lower edge

Making the gingham outfit

This pretty outfit will give your rag doll a truly traditional look. The blue and white gingham, long-sleeved dress is trimmed with broderie anglaise edging, and there is a gleaming white broderie anglaise pinafore to wear over the top.

All the pattern pieces include 1cm (³⁄₈in) seam allowances. Snip curves and corners and press the seam allowances open unless otherwise stated.

You will need

- 40cm (¹⁄₂yd) gingham fabric
- 30cm (³⁄₈yd) broderie anglaise fabric
- 1.5m (1⁵⁄₈yd) broderie anglaise edging, 2.5cm (1in) wide
- 50cm (⁵⁄₈yd) broderie anglaise edging, 7cm (2³⁄₄in) wide
- 1m (1¹⁄₈yd) satin ribbon, 1.5cm (⁵⁄₈in) wide
- White bias binding
- White sewing thread
- Two 1cm (³⁄₈in) snap fasteners

Making the pinafore

1 Cutting out Trace all the pattern pieces on to tracing paper, including the pattern marks, and cut out. Lay the pattern pieces on the fabric and cut the required number of each, placing pattern pieces to fold where indicated. Transfer all the marks with a dressmaker's pencil.

2 Neatening neck and armholes Right sides together, stitch back to front at shoulder seams. Right sides together, stitch one edge of bias binding to the armhole and neck edges. Stitch the side seams.

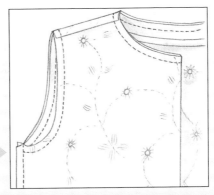

3 Trimming the hem Right sides together, stitch narrow broderie anglaise edging to the lower edge of the pinafore, and press the seam allowance towards the pinafore.

4 Attaching ribbon ties Cut the 1.5cm (⁵⁄₈in) wide ribbon into four. Matching raw edges, stitch two ribbons to the right side of the pinafore at each center back edge, positioning one at the neck edge and the other 5cm (2in) below.

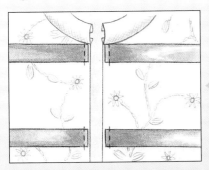

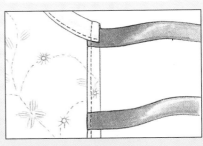

5 Finishing the pinafore Turn in and stitch a 6mm (¹⁄₄in) double hem down the back edges. At the neck and armholes, fold the bias binding to the wrong side and machine stitch in place.

▲ *For an old-fashioned style, choose traditional fabrics for your rag doll's outfit, such as fresh gingham and crisp broderie anglaise.*

Making the gingham dress

1 Stitching the shoulders Cut out the pattern pieces, as on page 37 step **1**. Then, right sides together, stitch the backs to the front at the shoulders.

2 Trimming the sleeves With right sides together, stitch narrow broderie anglaise edging to the lower edge of each sleeve. Then press the seam allowances towards the sleeves.

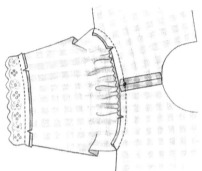

3 Stitching sleeves to dress Gather the top of the sleeve between the marks. Right sides together, pin the sleeves to the armholes, matching marks and placing the dots at the shoulder seams. Pull up the gathers to fit; stitch. Remove the gathering threads and press the seam allowances towards the sleeves.

4 Making the collar Cut a 47cm (18½in) length of the wide broderie anglaise edging. Turn under and stitch a 6mm (¼in) single hem at each short end.

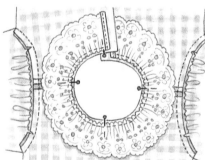

5 Stitching on the collar Gather the long raw edge of the collar, then divide it into four sections and mark with pins. With the right side of the collar to the wrong side of the dress, pin the collar to the neck edge, matching the pins to the shoulder seams and center front and back. Pull up the gathers to fit; tack, then stitch in place. Remove the tacking and gathering threads and turn the collar to the outside.

6 Stitching the sides With right sides together and armhole seams matching, stitch the back pieces to the front along the side and sleeve seams. Clip the curves.

7 Stitching back Stitch narrow broderie anglaise edging to the bottom edge of the dress, then press the seam allowances towards the dress. Stitch the center back seam from dot to hem. Snip to the dot at the top of the center back seam; press the seam open as far as the dot.

8 Finishing the back Turn in the seam allowances at the back opening by 6mm (¼in); stitch. Turn in the right-hand facing and overlap left-hand facing, matching center backs; press. Stitch on two snap fasteners, one just below neck edge and another about halfway down opening.

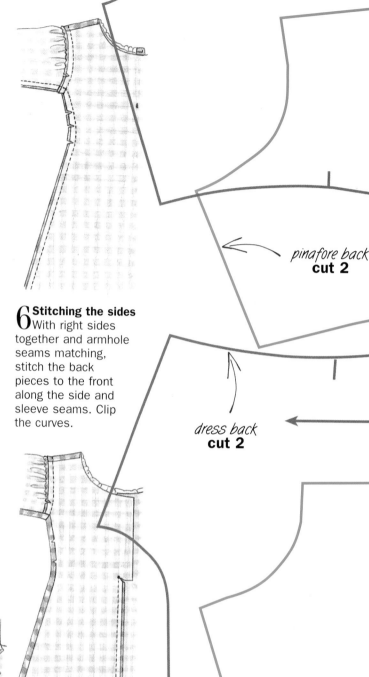

dress front
cut 1 on fold

pinafore back
cut 2

dress back
cut 2

pinafore front
cut 1 on fold

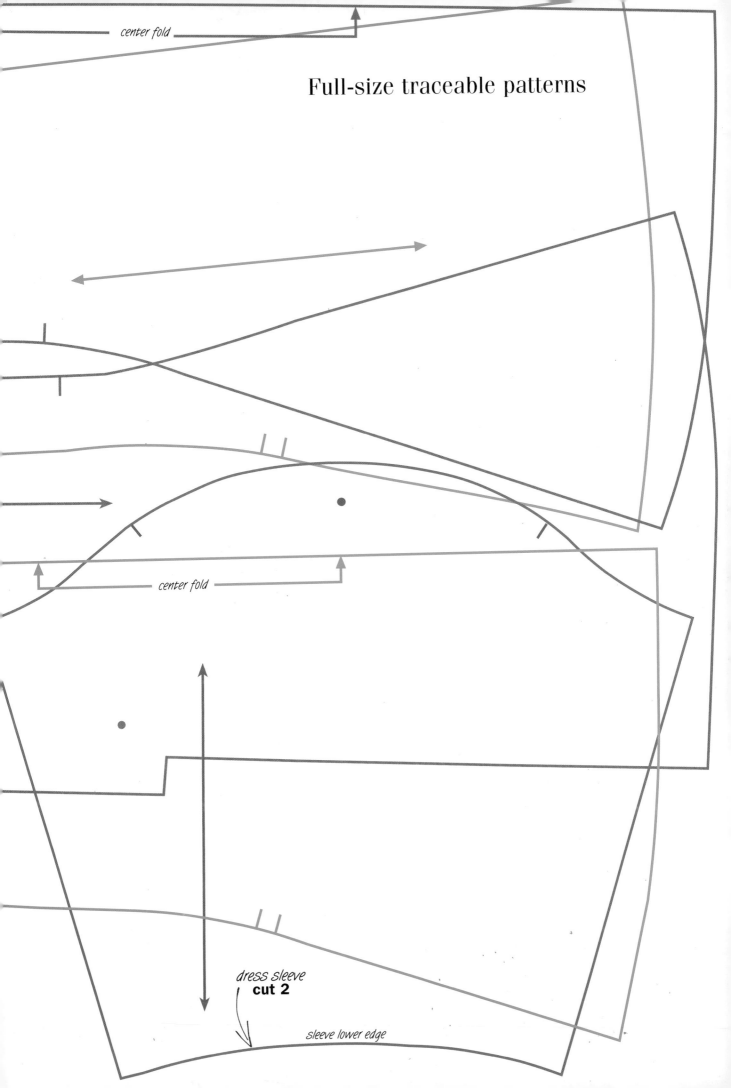

center fold

Full-size traceable patterns

center fold

dress sleeve
cut 2

sleeve lower edge

Making the ribbon-trimmed outfit

This stylish rag doll outfit features an eye-catching green pinafore trimmed with brightly colored ribbons, and a tie-dyed dress overprinted with flowers.

The neck frill is trimmed with ribbon to coordinate with the pinafore. Take 1cm (⅜) seams throughout; snip curves and corners and press the seams open.

Making the dress

1 Stitching the shoulders Cut out the pattern pieces as on page 37 step **1**. Stitch the backs to the front at the shoulders. Press the seams open.

You will need

- ◆ 50cm (⅝yd) lightweight printed cotton fabric
- ◆ 30cm (⅜yd) plain cotton fabric
- ◆ 1.5m (1⅝yd) satin ribbon in four widths: 3mm (⅛in), 8mm (⁵⁄₁₆in), 1cm (⅜in) and 1.5cm (⅝in)
- ◆ Matching bias binding
- ◆ Matching sewing thread
- ◆ Two 1cm (⅜in) snap fasteners

2 Stitching the sleeves Press 1cm (⅜in) to wrong side at lower edge of each sleeve. On the right side, stitch 8mm (⁵⁄₁₆in) wide ribbon, 6mm (¼in) above pressed edge. Stitch 3mm (⅛in) wide ribbon, 5mm (³⁄₁₆in) above first ribbon. Stitch sleeves to dress as on page 38 step **3**.

3 Making the collar Cut a strip of printed cotton fabric 47 x 8cm (18½ x 3¼in). Press 1cm (⅜in) to the wrong side on the long lower edge. On the right side, stitch 3mm (⅛in) wide ribbon, 6mm (¼in) above the pressed edge, then 1cm (⅜in) wide ribbon 5mm (³⁄₁₆in) above the first ribbon. Turn and stitch a narrow double hem on each short edge.

▼ *This stylish outfit uses bright fabrics and ribbon trims for a thoroughly modern look. It's cut from the same pattern pieces as the gingham outfit.*

4 Finishing off As on page 38 steps **5-6**, stitch on the collar and join the sides. As in steps **7-8**, stitch and finish the back, but omit the broderie anglaise edging. Press a 1cm (⅜in) hem at the bottom edge of the dress; stitch.

Making the pinafore

Follow the steps for *Making the pinafore* on page 37 but instead of trimming the lower edge with broderie anglaise, press a 1cm (⅜in) hem and stitch on three rows of ribbon in graduating widths, referring to step **2** above.

Hobby horse

*This friendly steed will delight the heart of
any child and give hours of fun, galloping from
one imaginary adventure to the next.*

The hobby horse is a traditional toy that has delighted children for generations and, despite the advent of electronic games, it still has as much appeal as ever. Though commercially made versions can be expensive, this do-it-yourself steed costs very little to put together and is not difficult to make. With its endearing personality, long sweeping eyelashes and well-groomed mane, it looks just as good as any hobby horse you can buy in a store, and it will quickly become a favorite companion for imaginative adventures.

The finished hobby horse is 84cm (33in) tall – just the right size for three to four-year-olds. For an older child, simply cut the pole longer. Choose a practical, durable fabric to make the horse's head. Any firm, plain cotton with a close weave, such as corded cotton or cotton gabardine, is suitable. Corduroy or heavy unbleached calico are excellent alternatives. If the hobby horse will be used for outdoor games, choose a darker color that won't show the dirt so easily.

◀ *Pausing just long enough for a quick photo-call, this little girl and her trusty companion will soon be off on another adventure together. For a bigger child, simply make the pole longer. For a more rugged looking steed, choose a dark corduroy and make the mane with thicker wool and no ribbons.*

Making the hobby horse

The pattern pieces for the head and ears of the hobby horse include a 1.5cm (⅝in) seam allowance. Toy safety eyes – an absolute must for young children – are available from most craft and needlework departments. The safest alternative, if you don't want to use these, is to embroider the eyes in satin stitch.

The stick 'body' part of the horse is a cut-down broom handle, which costs a great deal less than a length of strong dowelling, which is the other alternative. The flowing mane is made from lengths of wool, and the eyelashes and lids are cut from felt scraps, which are stiffened with glue. You will need grosgrain ribbon to make the bridle and reins, and satin ribbon for the ties on the mane. You will also need sewing threads to match the cotton fabric, the purple eyelids, the black eyelashes, the mane and the red flowers.

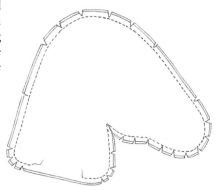

ear

You will need

- ◆ **40cm (½yd) of strong cotton fabric**
- ◆ **Scraps of black, lilac and red felt**
- ◆ **Mohair wool**
- ◆ **30 x 10cm (12 x 4in) 60g (2oz) polyester batting**
- ◆ **1.5m (1¾yd) of 1cm (⅜in) wide satin ribbon**
- ◆ **2m (2¼yd) of 1.5cm (⅝in) wide grosgrain ribbon**
- ◆ **Polyester toy filling**
- ◆ **Matching sewing threads**
- ◆ **Black embroidery floss**
- ◆ **Two toy safety eyes**
- ◆ **Tracing paper and pencil**
- ◆ **Dressmaker's pencil**
- ◆ **Wooden broom handle**
- ◆ **Red craft paint**
- ◆ **Latex glue**
- ◆ **Two small buttons**
- ◆ **Four small bells**

1 Preparing the pattern Trace off all the pattern pieces, including the pattern marks, given on these pages. Cut out and use them as patterns to cut out the fabric.

2 Cutting out *From cotton fabric:* fold the fabric in half to make a double layer and cut two heads and four ears. On both head pieces, mark the positions of the ears, eyes, mouth, nostrils and mane with a dressmaker's pencil. To strengthen the felt for the eyelids and lashes, smear one side of the black and lilac felt with glue and then leave to dry. *From lilac felt:* cut two eyelids. *From black felt:* cut two eyelashes. *From red felt:* cut four flowers.

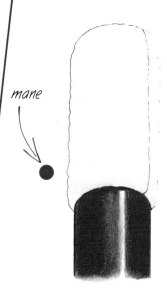

mane

5 Preparing the pole Cut the broom handle to 75cm (30in) long. Paint it red and leave it to dry. To stop the pole twisting inside the head, when attached, glue the batting strip around the sawn end.

3 Stitching the head With right sides together, stitch the two head pieces, taking a 1.5cm (⅝in) seam allowance and leaving an 8cm (3¼in) opening on the neck edge. Clip into the curves and the inner corner.

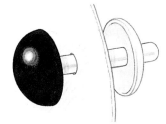

4 Positioning the eyes Cut a small hole at each eye position. From the right side, insert the stalk of a toy safety eye through each hole. On the wrong side, push the washer firmly on to the stalk to secure the eye in place.

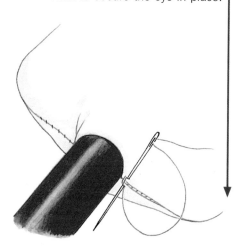

6 Fixing the head Turn the head right side out and stuff the muzzle and top of head with polyester toy filling. Push padded end of pole into the head and continue stuffing firmly. Slipstitch lower edges and oversew them each side of the pole to secure.

neck – lower edge

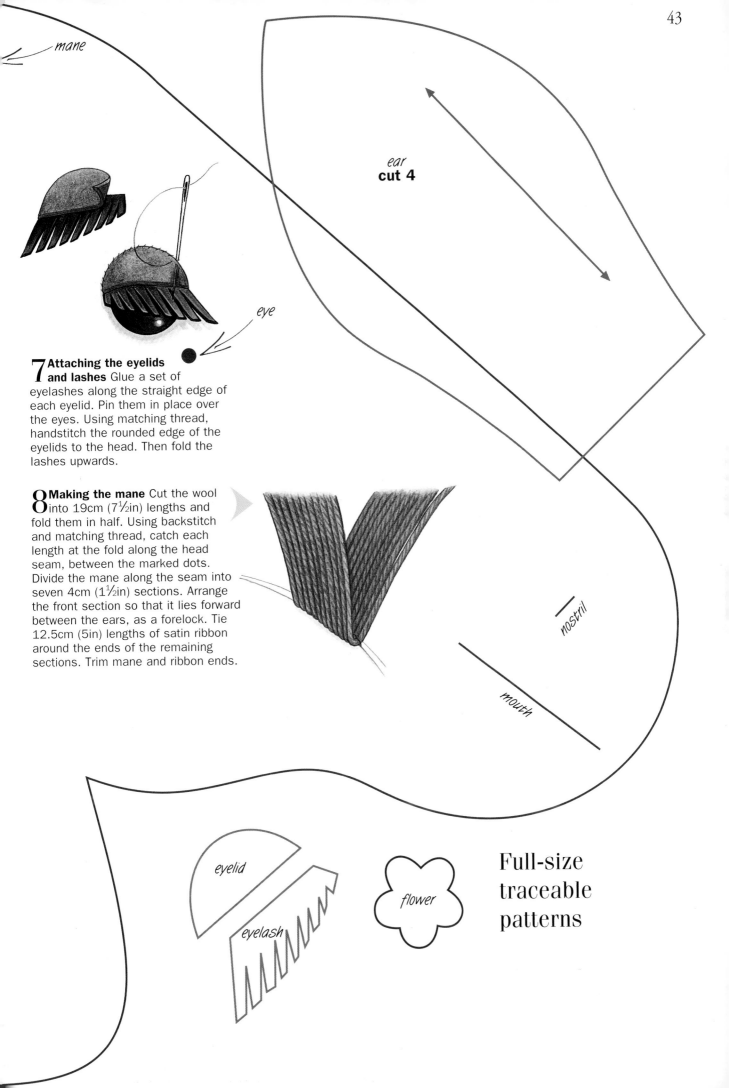

mane

ear
cut 4

eye

7 **Attaching the eyelids and lashes** Glue a set of eyelashes along the straight edge of each eyelid. Pin them in place over the eyes. Using matching thread, handstitch the rounded edge of the eyelids to the head. Then fold the lashes upwards.

8 **Making the mane** Cut the wool into 19cm (7½in) lengths and fold them in half. Using backstitch and matching thread, catch each length at the fold along the head seam, between the marked dots. Divide the mane along the seam into seven 4cm (1½in) sections. Arrange the front section so that it lies forward between the ears, as a forelock. Tie 12.5cm (5in) lengths of satin ribbon around the ends of the remaining sections. Trim mane and ribbon ends.

nostril

mouth

eyelid

eyelash

flower

Full-size
traceable
patterns

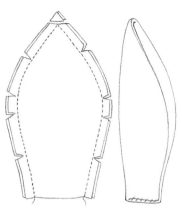

9 **Making the ears** With right sides together, stitch the ears in pairs, taking a 1.5cm (⅝in) seam allowance and leaving the lower edges open. Clip curves and corners, then turn to the right side. Turn in 1.5cm (⅝in) at the lower edges and slipstitch closed. Fold each ear in half and oversew lower edges together. Handstitch the ears securely to each side of the head at the marked positions.

10 **Making the bridle and reins** Pin grosgrain ribbon around the nose and cut off any excess ribbon, turning the raw ends under to neaten and butting them together. In the same way, pin the cheek straps and neck and head bands in position. Cut an 81cm (32in) length of ribbon for the reins and slip the raw ends under the nose strap; pin. With matching thread, sew the ribbons firmly to the head at the intersections.

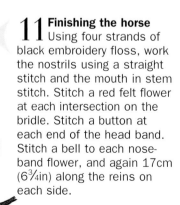

11 **Finishing the horse** Using four strands of black embroidery floss, work the nostrils using a straight stitch and the mouth in stem stitch. Stitch a red felt flower at each intersection on the bridle. Stitch a button at each end of the head band. Stitch a bell to each nose-band flower, and again 17cm (6¾in) along the reins on each side.

▲ *Jingling bells, bright buttons, felt flowers and ribbon bows, combined together, make an elegantly groomed steed. Mohair wool makes a lovely soft mane, but you could use almost any leftover knitting wool instead.*

Yo-Yo crocodile

The body of this friendly and cuddly yo-yo crocodile is soft and mobile. He is fun to make and irresistible to children of all ages.

These yo-yos are formed from small circles of fabric which are gathered round the outer edge and pulled up to create pretty circular puffs of material. Traditionally, they are sewn together and backed with fabric to make patchwork accessories for the home, such as bed covers or cushions. They can also be used singly to decorate fashion items or soft furnishings.

Alternatively, they can be threaded together to make delightful and endearing soft toys. What child could resist this friendly crocodile with his mischievous expression and delightfully mobile body? Cotton dress fabrics or lightweight furnishing cottons are ideal to use – they create puffs which hold their shape well, are easy to handle and are available in a huge variety of colors and designs. For added cuddle quality, the puffs for the crocodile are padded with lightweight polyester batting to give a softer feel.

▼ *Children will love this jolly yo-yo crocodile, and he's simple to make. The fabrics you choose for his body will enhance his personality – wacky patterns, checks and stripes will add to the fun.*

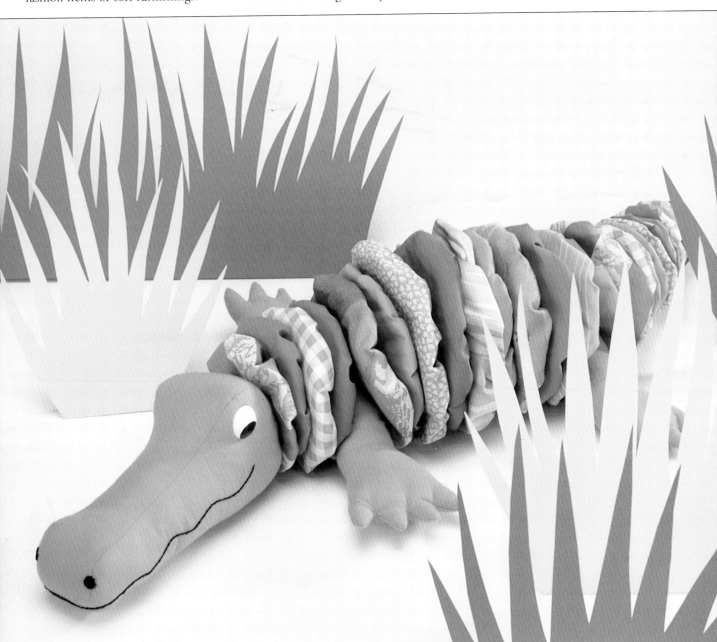

Making the crocodile

Choose a combination of nine different printed and plain fabrics to make the yo-yos, and another plain fabric for the head and legs. When assembling the crocodile's body and legs, make sure that you do not have two puffs of the same fabric side by side.

The finished crocodile measures about 67cm (26½in) long. The fabric quantities given are for 90cm (36in) wide fabrics. The pattern pieces for the head and legs include 1cm (⅜in) seam allowances. Clip all curves and press seams open, unless otherwise stated.

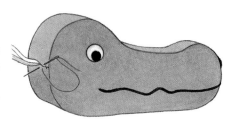

You will need

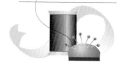

- 70cm (¾yd) of bright green cotton fabric
- 30cm (⅜yd) each of nine different cotton fabrics
- Two 2cm (¾in) diameter toy safety eyes
- 60cm (¾yd) of 50g (2oz) washable polyester batting
- Washable polyester toy filling
- 140cm (1⅝yd) of 6mm (¼in) wide elastic
- Black embroidery floss
- Matching thread
- Tracing paper and compass
- Bodkin

1 Cutting the head and legs Trace the pattern pieces from page 48, including markings, on to tracing paper and cut out. Tape together the tracings for gusset **A** and gusset **B** at dashed line. *From bright green fabric:* cut appropriate number of each piece.

2 Positioning the eyes Referring to page 42 step **4**, fix the safety eyes to the head sides at the marked positions.

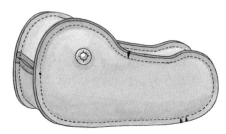

3 Stitching the head Press 1cm (⅜in) to the wrong side at each end of the gusset, then stitch the gusset between the head sides, matching the pressed edges to the dots. Turn through to the right side and stuff firmly with toy filling.

4 Finishing the head Using four strands of black embroidery floss in your needle, work the mouth in stem stitch and the nostrils in satin stitch. Cut two 60cm (23½in) lengths of elastic. Hold them together at one end and insert them into the head between the gusset ends. Handsew securely to the center of one pressed edge. Fasten off the thread securely, then oversew the gusset ends together.

5 Cutting the fabric circles *From the nine remaining fabrics:* referring to *Making a yo-yo* step **1**, cut the following: four 19cm (7½in) circles (**A**); four 22cm (8½in) circles (**B**); four 25cm (10in) circles (**C**); seven 28cm (11in) circles (**D**); three 16cm (6½in) circles (**E**); six 13cm (5in) circles (**F**); and one 10cm (4in) circle (**G**). Label the circles clearly and put to one side.

6 Cutting the batting circles *From the batting:* referring to *Making a yo-yo* step **1**, cut the following: four 9.5cm (3¾in) circles; four 11cm (4¼in) circles; four 12.5cm (5in) circles; seven 14cm (5½in) circles; three 8cm (3¼in) circles; six 6.5cm (2½in) circles; and one 5cm (2in) circle. Label the circles clearly.

Making a Yo-Yo

Cut the fabric circles accurately using paper templates. To draw the templates, use a compass for smaller circles and a pin and tape measure for larger ones; or draw round household objects, such as jars and eggcups.

1 Making the template Halve the diameter of the circle – this is the radius. *Using a compass:* set the compass to the radius measurement, draw the circle on paper and cut out. *Using a tape measure:* pin the tape to the paper at the radius measurement. Hold a pencil at the end, keep the tape taut, then swivel the end of the tape round the pin to mark a circle.

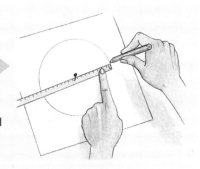

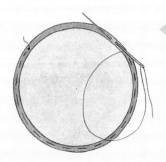

2 Preparing fabric Pin the template to the fabric and cut out. Finger press a 3mm (⅛in) hem all round the fabric circle. Then work small gathering stitches all round the circle, close to the folded edge.

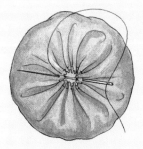

3 Finishing the yo-yo Pull up the gathering stitches tightly to gather the circle of fabric into a yo-yo. Fasten off the thread securely.

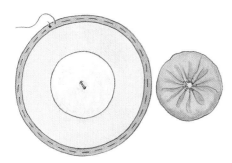

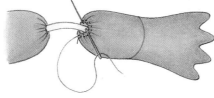

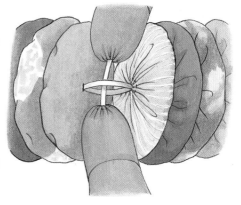

7 **Making the yo-yos** On the wrong side of each fabric circle, center a batting circle half its diameter; pin to hold, placing the pin on the right side of the fabric. Then make the yo-yo as in *Making a yo-yo* steps **2-3**, pulling up the gathering threads tightly to enclose the batting; remove pins.

10 **Attaching the leg elastics** Cut one 5.5cm (2⅛in) length of elastic. Insert one end of the elastic into a leg; pull up the gathering thread tightly and handstitch it securely to the elastic. Then insert the other end of the elastic into another leg in the same way to make a pair. Repeat to join the two remaining legs.

12 **Inserting the legs** Slip one pair of legs through the body elastics, positioning it between the fourth and fifth yo-yos. Ease the yo-yos back into position to conceal the leg elastic. Repeat to insert the second pair of legs between the thirteenth and fourteenth yo-yos.

13 **Securing the yo-yos** Push the yo-yos along the body elastics. Trim the elastics, leaving 1cm (⅜in) extending. Handstitch the elastic ends securely to the wrong side of the remaining yo-yo (**G**).

8 **Preparing the legs** Press 1cm (⅜in) to the wrong side on the short, straight edge of the leg fronts and the leg and foot backs. With right sides together, place the curved edge of each leg front to a foot front; pin to hold. Stitch between the dots.

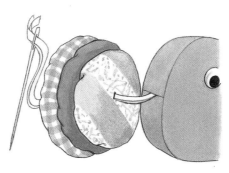

11 **Assembling the crocodile** Set aside the smallest yo-yo (**G**). Cut a small hole in the center of the other yo-yos. Thread the head elastics on to a bodkin. With right sides facing the head, thread the yo-yos on to the elastic in the following order: two **A**; two **B**; two **C**; seven **D**; two **C**; two **B**; two **A**; three **E**; and six **F**.

▼ *As it's held together with a length of elastic, running from its head to its tail, you can pull the crocodile and it stretches; let it go and it pings back into shape.*

9 **Making legs and feet** With right sides together and matching dots on side seams, pin leg and foot fronts to leg and foot backs. Leaving pressed edges open, stitch, working through dots between toes. Snip seam allowances to the dots. Turn to right side and work a row of gathering stitches close to pressed seams. Stuff firmly.

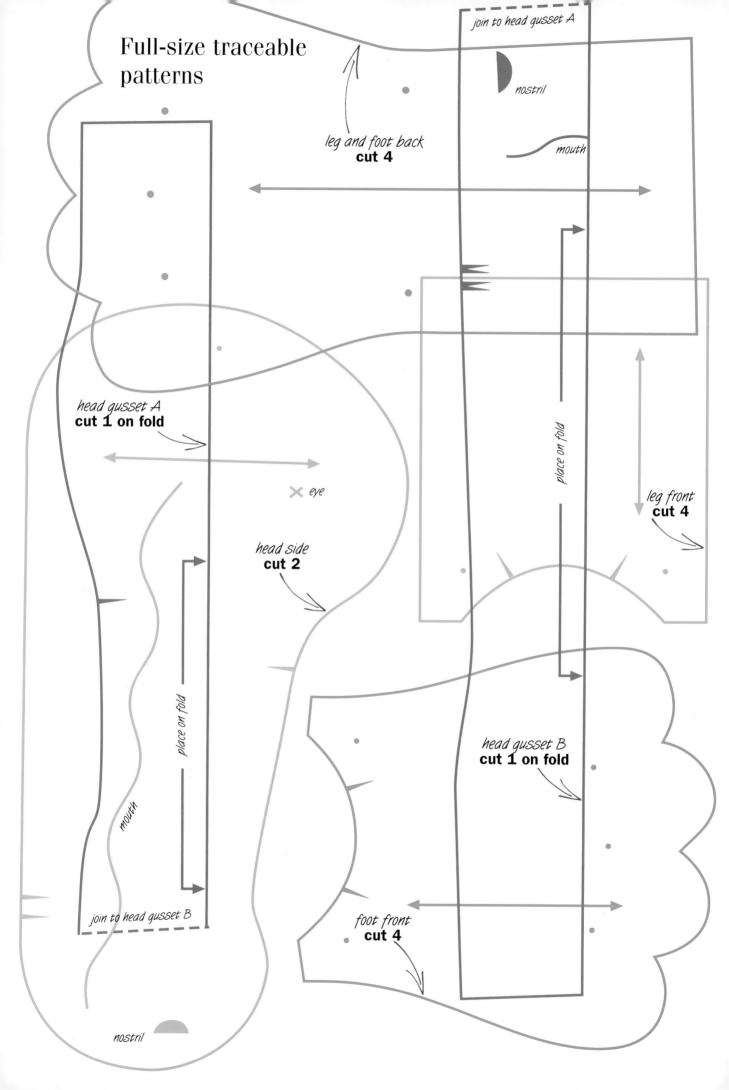

Full-size traceable
patterns

join to head gusset A

nostril

mouth

leg and foot back
cut 4

head gusset A
cut 1 on fold

× eye

place on fold

leg front
cut 4

head side
cut 2

place on fold

head gusset B
cut 1 on fold

mouth

join to head gusset B

foot front
cut 4

nostril

Child's tepee

*Give your children hours of fun with this portable play house –
a simple tepee in bright cotton fabrics to put up easily on any soft ground. They can
even help you to decorate it with easy shapes cut with pinking shears.*

Children always love the idea of their own little house, and a tepee has the added appeal of the Wild West. The tepee is quick to put up – it is supported by poles you just push into the ground. When not in use, it rolls up to store away, so you can easily take it on vacation.

The tepee is simple to make. It consists of six fabric triangles stitched together, with bamboo poles slotted into casings at each seam. Have fun with the children cutting random decorative shapes to appliqué on – triangles and rectangles are easy and effective, or try a moon or two.

One triangle is split in two to make an opening, with chunky toggle fixings to suit small fingers, so the entrance can either be closed up or fixed open.

▲ *Pinking the edges of the seams and appliqué motifs makes the tepee a speedy project to put together, and adds to the decorative effect.*

We used a cotton twill in three brilliant colors, but you could use creamy calico or canvas and brighten it with appliqué scraps, or use a different fabric for each panel and the appliqué motifs.

Making the tepee

Make sure you buy fabric which is at least 129cm (50¾in) wide. If you can find fabric 150cm (59in) wide, you will have enough offcuts to make the mat described on page 52.

You will need

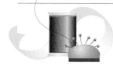

- ◆ **Three x 1.75m (2yd) firm cotton fabric, in different colors, at least 129cm (50¾in) wide**

- ◆ **Matching thread**

- ◆ **Five large wooden toggles**

- ◆ **2.5m (2¾yd) colored cord, 1cm (⅜in) diameter**

- ◆ **Bonding fabric**

- ◆ **Paper for pattern**

- ◆ **Pinking shears**

- ◆ **Tailor's chalk**

- ◆ **Six x 183cm (6ft) long bamboo poles**

▶ *The tepee is made up of six panels, cut in three alternating colors for maximum contrast and impact. Bright, vibrant colors are fun, or choose three pastel shades for a more muted look.*

9cm (3½in)

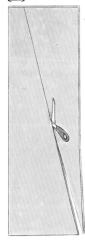

1 Making the pattern Cut a piece of paper 129cm (50¾in) long by 82cm (32¼in) wide, and fold in half lengthways. At one end, measure and mark a point 9cm (3½in) from the fold. Draw a straight line from this point to the bottom outer corner, and trim off excess. Open out.

2 Cutting out Use the pattern to cut two pieces in the first two colors, and one in the third, with the foldline on the straight grain. For the door flaps, fold the pattern lengthways, and cut two pieces in the third color, adding 4cm (1½in) at the folded edge of the pattern.

3 Hemming the edges On the shorter ends of each, turn under 1cm then 1cm (⅜in then ⅜in) hem, and stitch, using a contrasting color. On each doorflap, at the center edge, turn under 1cm then 2.5cm (⅜in then 1in) hem, and stitch.

4 Joining the door flaps Right sides up, overlap the center hemmed edges by 6mm (¼in) and pin. Starting at the top, top stitch through all thicknesses for 15cm (6in), reversing at each end for strength.

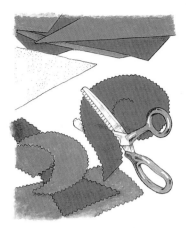

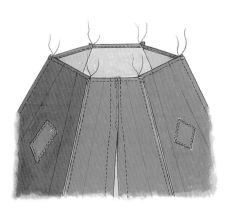

5 Preparing the decorative shapes Fuse bonding fabric to the wrong side of remnants of the fabrics, following the manufacturer's instructions. Cut out about 30 decorative shapes – triangles and rectangles are easy, or try moons or spirals for a change. Trim the edges with pinking shears.

6 Stitching the appliqué On the right side, chalk a line 6cm (2¼in) from the raw edges of each section. Arrange five appliqué motifs on each section, within the lines, and fuse in place with a hot iron. In contrast thread, straight stitch round each motif, 6mm (¼in) in from the edge.

7 Joining the seams Wrong sides together, pin the raw edge of one doorflap to the side edge of a contrasting section. Continue adding contrasting sections in the same way, finishing with the remaining doorflap. Stitch, taking a 2cm (¾in) seam allowance.

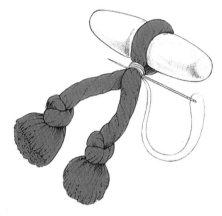

8 Making the casings On each join, stitch again along the chalked lines, reversing at top and bottom to reinforce. With the pinking shears, trim a tiny amount off the seam allowances, leaving a neatly pinked edge.

9 Making the toggle fastenings Cut ten pieces of cord 22cm (8¾in) long. Tie a knot 1cm (⅜in) from each end, and fray out to make a tassel. Fold one length round each toggle, fastening tightly by winding double thread tightly round, then stitching through the cord.

10 Securing the toggles On the right side, position one toggle at the bottom corner of one of the doorflaps, sticking out from the edge, and stitch the cord securely in place, halfway between the toggle and tassels. Space three other toggles evenly up the edge.

11 Adding the loops Fold the remaining pieces of tasseled cord in two to make loops. On the other door flap, pin a loop opposite each toggle, overhanging the edge so that the toggles can be pushed through. Stitch securely as for the toggles.

12 Finishing off To secure the flaps in the open position, fold back each flap as far as the casing, right sides together, and stitch the last toggle and loop to correspond with those on the bottom corners. Push the poles through the casings, pushing the bottom ends into the ground.

▲ The tepee closes up snugly with a series of rope loops and toggles that can be fastened from inside or outside. Each rope end is knotted and frayed, creating a row of tiny tassels.

Crazy play mat

This colorful play mat is a great way to put offcuts of fabric to good use. Pinked at the edges and overlapped in a crazy patchwork pattern, the offcuts make a circular play mat which will fit inside the wigwam, serve as a base on the beach, or as a cloth for a picnic. It has a waterproof nylon backing so you don't have to worry about damp grass – and you can use it for children's tea parties indoors, to protect your carpet.

It is quick and easy to make. The shapes you start with determine the design, so don't worry too much – the children will like it as long as it's colorful. We used offcuts from the tepee but you could use any other large pieces of sturdy fabric. A deep pinked fringe (we used felt) runs around the edge of the mat. The finished diameter is 136cm (53½in) including the fringe.

▲ *Overlapping leftover offcuts of fabric form a random patchwork effect – the shapes of the pieces you use will determine the design.*

You will need

- ◆ **Offcuts of fabric for mat**
- ◆ **41cm (16in) fabric or felt for fringe**
- ◆ **1.5m (1⅝yd) waterproof nylon fabric (such as shower curtaining) for backing**
- ◆ **Contrasting threads**
- ◆ **Newspaper for pattern**
- ◆ **Pinking shears**
- ◆ **Pencil**
- ◆ **Measuring tape**

1 Cutting the backing Fold the backing in four and make a 120cm (47¼in) circle as follows. Wrap one end of a length of string around a pencil and the other end around the drawing pin so that the length of the taut string is the radius of the mat. Holding the pencil upright, draw a quarter circle on the paper. Open out.

2 Preparing the fabrics Iron the offcuts and trim off any small projections or awkward curves. Trim all the edges with the pinking shears.

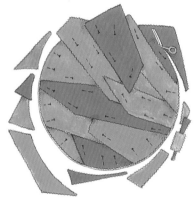

3 Assembling the design Right side up, lay the pieces on the nylon circle, overlapping all edges by at least 2cm (¾in), until the whole circle is covered. Adjust as desired, balancing colors and shapes, and pin securely. Trim the edges level with the nylon, using the pinking shears.

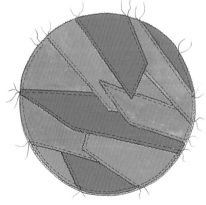

4 Stitching the design Using contrasting threads, stitch all the edges 1cm (⅜in) in from the pinked edge; stitch round the outer edge in the same way.

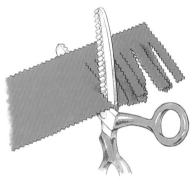

5 Making the fringe With pinking shears, cut the fringe fabric into enough 10cm (4in) wide strips to go all round the edge of the mat. Make 7cm (2¾in) cuts 1cm (⅜in) apart along one edge of all the strips.

6 Applying the fringe Pleating slightly to follow the curve, pin the strips round the mat edge, overlapping it by 2cm (¾in), and overlapping strip ends to join. Stitch, 1cm (⅜in) in.

Christmas stockings

For children, there's no better way of anticipating Christmas than hanging up their own, specially made stockings and waiting for them to be filled with gifts.

Much of the spirit of Christmas lies in the anticipation and preparation: making presents, and decorations and planning menus in advance. For children, it's a time for writing lists to Santa and happy hours playing with glitter and tinsel. One event, which once tried is sure to become an annual ritual, is hanging up the Christmas stockings. Children may hang them up a week or so beforehand, expecting them to be filled with gifts on Christmas morning.

You will enjoy creating these jolly stockings. They are made in easy-to-sew felt, and instructions for two different designs are given on the following pages; one with spots and one with stripes. They are lined to help keep their shape and to make them more durable.

▲ *The stockings are roomy enough to hold plenty of toys, wrapped or unwrapped. You can add further embellishments to the stockings, such as the ribbon bows shown here. To avoid any arguments on the day, why not stitch or appliqué the name of each recipient on the stocking cuff?*

Spotted stocking

This jolly stocking is made from felt sold by the meter (yard), and the spots are made from felt circles. You can buy felt on the roll from fabric stores.

You will need

- 60cm (¾yd) of orange felt
- 60cm (¾yd) of 90cm (36in) wide fabric for lining
- 10cm (4in) of blue felt
- One 20cm (8in) square each of red, yellow and green felt
- 20cm (8in) of 1cm (⅜in) wide ribbon for loop
- Dressmaker's pattern paper
- Flexicurve (optional)
- Matching thread
- Compass and pencil
- Dressmaker's pencil

Scaling up the pattern

It's easy to draw up this tiny, scaled-down version of the stocking pattern to the full size. There are three alternative ways of doing this:

Dressmaker's paper This is sold specifically for scaling up patterns and you can buy it from most fabric stores.

Drawing up a grid Draw up a grid of 2cm (¾in) wide squares on to a large sheet of paper, such as the reverse side of a piece of wallpaper. In addition to the materials listed, you will need a set square and a long ruler.

Photocopy Keep enlarging the pattern until the length of the stocking measures 59cm (23¼in).

SCALE FOR PATTERN

One square = 2cm (¾in)

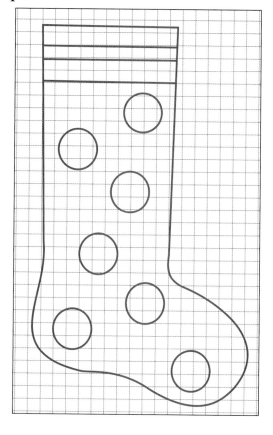

---

1 Scaling up the pattern Starting at the top left-hand corner of both the stocking pattern and the grid paper, use a pencil to plot the points where the stocking outline crosses a square. Join the points freehand or use the flexicurve for the curved parts. Use the compass and pencil to draw on 6cm (2¼in) circles at the positions indicated on the pattern.

2 Cutting out *From the orange felt and lining fabric:* cut two complete stockings from both fabrics and two 22 x 2cm (8¾ x ¾in) strips from the orange felt only, for the cuff trim. *From the blue felt:* cut two 22 x 9cm (8¾ x 3½in) cuffs. *For the circles:* cut two 8cm (3⅛in) diameter circles from the blue felt and four each from the red, green and yellow felt.

3 Marking circles on the stocking Cut the circles out of the paper stocking pattern. Lay the pattern over each orange felt stocking and, using the dressmaker's pencil, draw around the inside of each circle. Cut out the circles from the felt stocking.

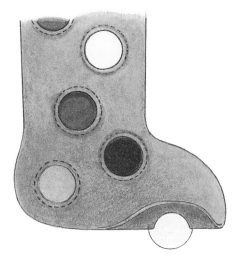

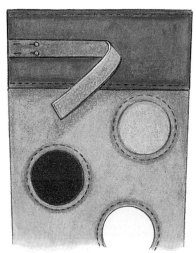

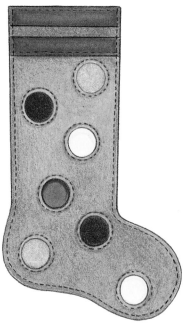

4 Stitching the circles Position a felt circle behind each cut-out circle on the stocking, with the edges overlapping evenly all around. Working from the right side, pin, tack, and then topstitch the circles in place.

5 Stitching the cuffs Pin and tack a blue cuff across the top edge of each stocking piece, with top and side edges level. Topstitch in place across top and lower edges. Place an orange strip across the center of each blue cuff; pin and tack at each end only.

6 Assembling the felt stocking With wrong sides facing, pin and tack the two stocking pieces together around the side and lower edges. Then topstitch 6mm (¼in) in from the edge.

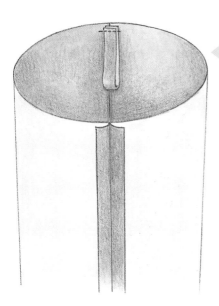

7 Assembling the lining With right sides together, stitch the lining pieces together at the side and lower edges, taking 6mm ($\frac{1}{4}$in) seams. Press seams open along straight part of leg. Fold the ribbon into a loop. Pin the loop to right side of lining at the center back seam, with raw edges level and loop pointing downwards. Stitch 6mm ($\frac{1}{4}$in) from fabric edge.

8 Assembling the stocking Press 6mm ($\frac{1}{4}$in) to the wrong side around the top edge of the lining so that the loop projects upwards. Place the lining inside the stocking, wrong sides together. Pin pressed top edge of lining level with the cuff stitching. Slipstitch lining to cuff stitching.

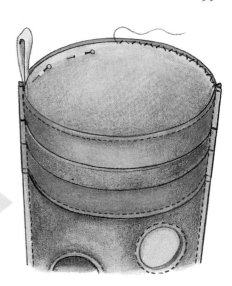

▶ *Multi-colored spots adorn this bright orange stocking. You can hang the stockings from a hook or bed knob using the ribbon loop stitched securely between the main stocking and the lining.*

Striped stocking

You need five different colors of felt for this stocking: one for the main stocking, two for the cuff and two for the stripes. Due to the width required, you will need to buy felt by the meter (yard) for all the pieces. Use the colors suggested here, or try a more traditional combination of red, green and gold.

You will need

- ◆ 60cm (³⁄₄yd) of yellow felt
- ◆ 20cm (¹⁄₄yd) each of blue and orange felt
- ◆ 10cm (¹⁄₈yd) each of green and red felt
- ◆ 60cm (³⁄₄yd) of 90cm (36in) wide fabric for lining
- ◆ 20cm (8in) of 1cm (³⁄₈in) wide ribbon for loop
- ◆ Matching thread

1 Cutting out Scale up the stocking pattern as in step **1** on page 54. *From the yellow felt and lining:* cut two complete stocking shapes from each. *From orange felt:* cut two 22 x 9cm (8³⁄₄ x 3¹⁄₂in) cuffs. *From the blue felt:* Cut four 22 x 9cm (8³⁄₄ x 3¹⁄₂in) strips and two 36 x 9cm (14¹⁄₄ x 3¹⁄₂in) strips. *From the green, red and orange felt:* cut two 5cm (2in) wide strips from each color to fit across the center of the blue strips.

◄ This striped stocking is made by cutting a stocking shape from yellow felt; then the blue strips are stitched on top, with the green, red and orange strips on top of these.

2 Stitching the cuff Pin and tack an orange cuff to the top edge of each stocking piece, making sure that the top and side edges are level. Then topstitch the cuff in place across the top and lower edges.

3 Stitching on the blue strips Pin one of the shorter blue strips across the stocking, with its top edge 6cm (2¹⁄₄in) below the cuff. Pin a long blue strip with its lower edge level with the heel. Pin a shorter strip in place midway between the other two. Trim strips level with stocking edges. Tack, then zigzag stitch in place, across the top and lower edges of the strips.

4 Adding the center strips Pin and tack the green, red and orange strips centrally along the blue strips. Trim them level with the stocking edges and then zigzag stitch in place across top and lower edges. Complete the stocking as in steps **6-8** on pages 54–55.

Christmas patchwork

The craft of patchwork has many unusual and unexpected applications, such as these festive cards and hangings. Made from tiny fabric scraps, they are Christmas gifts to treasure.

Christmas is the time of year when old traditions compete for space with tinsel, glitter and sparkle. These greetings cards combine the best of both seasonal elements, using an old and very traditional patchwork design to display contemporary Christmas fabrics, with lots of emphasis on festive shimmer and shine.

The patchwork is based on the Ohio Star block. In the original version of this design, a series of squares and triangles are stitched together. But in the version shown here, squares and strips of fabric are folded into smaller squares, rectangles and triangles, and then layered on top of each other, creating a design which has plenty of depth and texture.

The same patchwork design, backed with a decorative fabric and trimmed with shiny beads, makes a special festive hanging. Give one to your friends to

▲ *It's always delightful to receive homemade greetings cards, and these patchwork Christmas cards are particularly charming. Combine seasonal prints with festive gold lamé to make your season's greetings all the more special.*

hang on the Christmas tree – it's child friendly, so it won't break. Make one for your family tree or let it dangle from the mantelpiece, a shelf, or even a doorknob.

Making the cards

The patchwork block uses four fabrics. For festive glitter, use a gold or silver lamé, and combine it with three other coordinating or contrasting designs in traditional Christmas colors, such as red and green. For the best effect, use light to mediumweight, firmly woven fabrics that hold a crease well. You will also need a background fabric. Calico is ideal, but you could use any firmly woven fabric, as long as it has plenty of body.

To complete the gift, use a three-fold greetings card blank with a 7.5cm (3in) window. You can buy these at art and craft suppliers, some stationery stores, or mail order suppliers. Alternatively, you can make your own card blanks from thin card, as shown opposite.

1 Preparing the background Using a dressmaker's pencil, measure and mark the center of each edge of the calico square. Using a ruler, draw lines between opposite marks – where they cross is the center of the square. Draw lines 6mm (¼in) away from each marked line on either side.

2 Cutting out Measure and mark the fabric pieces carefully before cutting out, to ensure accuracy. *From fabric A:* cut four 5cm (2in) squares. *From fabric B:* cut four 5cm (2in) squares. *From gold or silver lamé:* cut four 9 x 5cm (3½ x 2in) strips. *From fabric C:* cut eight 5cm (2in) squares.

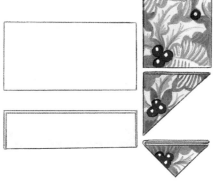

3 Folding the squares Take all the fabric A and B squares, and four of the fabric C squares. Fold each of these squares in half with the wrong sides together; then fold each one in half again to form a 2.5cm (1in) square. Finger press along the folds or press lightly with an iron.

4 Folding the strips and triangles Fold the gold or silver lamé strips in half lengthways, with wrong sides together. Press. Fold the remaining fabric C squares in half diagonally, with wrong sides together; fold them in half again to form triangles. Finger press or press lightly with an iron.

5 Adding the first squares On the background square, place two A squares and two B squares, folded corner to the center, as shown. Using matching thread, secure each square at the center with a tiny stitch – make sure it doesn't show from the front. Then stitch round the squares, 3mm (⅛in) from the outside edges.

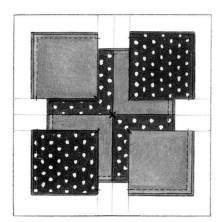

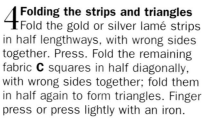

6 Adding the next layer Place an A square over each B square, 6mm (¼in) from the center, using marked lines as a guide. Repeat to place a B square over each original A square. Secure the squares as in step **5**.

7 Adding the strips Place a folded gold or silver lamé strip along each side of the background square, with raw edges matching; secure with a tiny stitch at each inner corner. Stitch 3mm (⅛in) from the outside edges.

8 Completing the design Place a C square at each corner, then center a C triangle along each edge. Secure the shapes in place as before. To finish the patchwork design, stitch a gold bead to the center.

▲ *These patchwork cards are based on the Ohio Star block, but instead of stitching the shapes together, they are layered on top of one another to give depth and textural appeal. Experiment with different fabrics for the best effects.*

Making a card blank

If you have difficulty finding a card blank to set off your Ohio Star, make your own using a 33 x 15cm (13 x 6in) piece of brightly colored card or shiny metallic cardstock. The key to success is accurate cutting with the craft knife, so before you try the real thing, practice using the knife on a scrap of card. You can buy sheets of card and craft knives in art stores and some stationery stores.

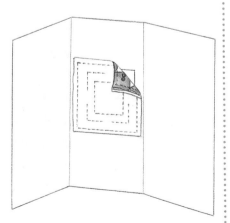

9 Making the card Center the Ohio Star, face down, in the aperture on the inside of the greetings card. Turn the card over to check the positioning, then glue in place. Glue inside flap of the card over back of the patchwork.

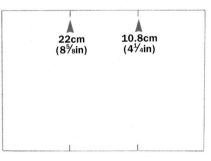

▲ 22cm (8⅝in)   ▲ 10.8cm (4¼in)

1 Preparing the card Along both long edges of the rectangle, measure and mark lightly 10.8cm (4¼in) from one short edge. Mark again 22cm (8⅝in) from the same edge.

2 Scoring the folds Hold the ruler vertically between the first two marks. Using the blunt edge of the craft knife, score lightly along the edge of the ruler. Repeat to score between the next two marks.

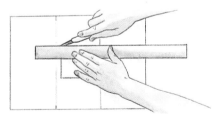

3 Cutting out the window Place the card with the scored side up. In the center of the middle section, between the scored lines, draw a 7.5cm (3in) square. Rest the card on a cutting surface, and cut out the window section, running the knife against the edge of the ruler.

4 Folding the card Erase all the pencil marks carefully. Then fold the card, making sure that the scored side is on the outside.

Making a hanging

These colorful festive hangings are simply folded Ohio Star square blocks, hung with beads and bells, and backed with a square of fabric, which is folded neatly around the edges of the block. Cut this square from the fabric **C** used in the patchwork, or use a different fabric that coordinates with the other four.

You will need

- ◆ **Folded Ohio Star square block**
- ◆ **12.5cm (5in) square of fabric C**
- ◆ **Two or three small beads**
- ◆ **Bell or drop bead**
- ◆ **20cm (8in) narrow ribbon or cord**
- ◆ **Matching threads**

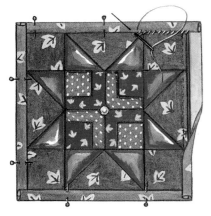

1 Backing the block Center the folded Ohio Star block on the backing square, wrong sides together. Fold the edges of the backing square over the edges of the block, turning them under neatly; pin and press. Slipstitch the edges in place.

2 Adding the beads Secure a length of thread at one corner of the hanging. Bring the needle out at the tip of the corner. Thread on two small beads and a drop bead, then take the thread back up through the beads and secure it .

3 Adding the hanging loop Fold the cord or ribbon in half. Position it on the wrong side of the hanging, on the corner diagonally opposite the beads. Stitch securely in place.

▲ *Make a patchwork hanging to trim the Christmas tree.*

For a hanging, make any number of hanging folded Ohio Star patchwork blocks, stitch them on to a length of matching ribbon, and sew a hanging ring at the top of the ribbon.

Christmas baubles

*Based on traditional patchwork shapes, these colorful
beaded decorations will bring glitter and detail to a Christmas
tree. They are easy to make and will last for years.*

Handmade tree decorations are the perfect way to give the Christmas tree a traditional, homey look, and they make welcome gifts for friends and family. They use only tiny pieces of fabric, so your main investment will be beads, bead trims and embroidery floss. Don't be afraid to splash out on these little extras – unlike many other tree decorations, made from rather fragile materials such as colored glass, these fabric and bead baubles are practically unbreakable, so

they'll last for years. They are also very lightweight, so can be used to decorate small trees without fear of bending or snapping the branches.

Each design is based on a traditional patchwork shape – choose from the long hexagon, the hexagon, and the romantic heart. A paper backing gives body to each fabric panel, and the panels are either joined together with decorative stitching or trimmed with beading. For a festive touch, strings of glittering beads dangle from the base of each bauble.

All the designs are very easy to make and assemble. The stitching is done by hand, and even if you are not an experienced needleworker, you will quickly master the techniques involved.

▼ *The Christmas tree takes on a traditional look with these pretty fabric baubles. Each one is based on a popular patchwork shape, expressed in three dimensions and decorated with glittery beads for that essential festive touch.*

Making the baubles

Aim to make your baubles as bright and glittery as possible. Use a variety of Christmas fabrics in traditional festive shades of red and green, decorated with gold highlights. Avoid fabrics with large designs – mini prints are ideal. For the beads, select a mixture of red and gold in a range of sizes, and choose basting floss in red, green or gold. You can buy beads, bells and other trims in fabric stores or from mail order suppliers.

You will need

- ◆ **Christmas fabrics**
- ◆ **Embroidery floss**
- ◆ **Selection of beads, including drop beads and strung beads**
- ◆ **Bells (optional)**
- ◆ **Needle and sewing thread**
- ◆ **Thin card**
- ◆ **Cartridge paper**
- ◆ **Tracing paper**
- ◆ **Scissors**

Long hexagon

Based on the long hexagon shape, this bauble uses four pieces to achieve its three-dimensional effect. Without the beads it is 7.5cm (3in) high.

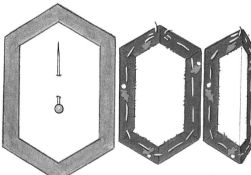

1 Cutting out the paper shapes Trace the long hexagon, given on page 64, on to card. Cut it out to make a card template. On cartridge paper, draw around template four times and cut out the shapes.

2 Cutting out the fabric On fabric, center a card template on your chosen motif and draw around it, adding a 1cm (⅜in) seam allowance all around; cut out the shape. Repeat to cut three more fabric hexagons.

3 Preparing the pieces Center and pin a paper hexagon on wrong side of each fabric shape. Fold the seam allowances over edges of paper; tack to hold. Fold each paper-backed piece in half lengthways, right sides together.

Triple hexagon

Each hexagon shape is made from three separate pieces joined together. The large hexagon measures 5cm (2in) high, the medium one is 4cm (1½in) high and the small hexagon is 3cm (1¼in) high.

1 **Cutting out the pieces** Trace the large, medium and small hexagons on to card and cut them out to make card templates. On cartridge paper, draw around each template three times and cut them out. As in *Long hexagon* step **2**, cut out three small, three medium and three large hexagon shapes from fabric.

2 **Joining the pieces** Prepare the fabric and join the three small hexagon pieces, as for *Long hexagon* steps **3-4**, leaving the last edge unstitched. Repeat to make the medium and large hexagons.

3 **Threading the base beads** Using all six strands of a 65cm (25in) length of embroidery floss, thread the base beads on to the small hexagon, as in *Long hexagon* step **5**.

4 **Joining the shapes** Secure the thread at the inside top of the small hexagon, then thread on two or three more beads. Repeat to join on the medium and large hexagons. Make the hanger and finish off following *Long hexagon* steps **6-7**.

◀ Make your patchwork baubles from scraps of leftover fabric in traditional Christmas red, green and gold.

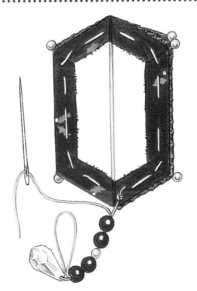

4 **Joining the pieces** Place two pieces wrong sides together. Using three strands of embroidery floss and glove stitch, as shown on page 64, stitch the pieces together along one side edge, working from the top to the bottom and adding a bead at each side corner. Repeat to add the other three pieces, but leave the last edge unstitched.

5 **Threading the base beads** Thread a needle with all six strands of a 50cm (20in) length of embroidery floss. Work a few small stitches to secure thread inside base of ornament. Thread on the beads, finishing with a bell loop or a drop bead. Then pass the thread back up through beads and secure on inside of base.

6 **Making the hanger** Take the thread up to the top and thread on more beads. Take the needle back through the beads, leaving a 7.5cm (3in) loop of thread above them; secure the thread ends on the inside. Knot the thread just above the beads.

7 **Finishing off** Stitch the last side edge as before, adding a bead at each corner. To complete the ornament, remove all the tacking stitches.

Double hearts

Each heart is made of three separate hearts, and the seams are trimmed with strung beads. You'll need about 40cm (16in) of strung bead trim for the large heart, and 27cm (11in) for the small one. The large heart is 7cm (2¾in) high and the small one 4.5cm (1¾in) high.

1 Cutting out Trace the small and large hearts on to card and cut out to make templates. On cartridge paper, draw around each heart template three times and cut out. Cut three small and three large hearts from fabric, as in *Long hexagon* step **2**. Then prepare the pieces, as in *Long hexagon* step **3**.

2 Joining the pieces *For the small heart*, cut a 27cm (11in) length of bead trim. Wrong sides together and starting at the top, oversew two hearts together along one side edge, catching in the trim as you stitch. Add the third heart at the bottom, and continue to catch in trim. At the top, secure the thread but do not cut off the trim. *For the large heart*, repeat, using a 40cm (16in) length of bead trim.

3 Stringing the pieces Thread on the base beads as in *Long hexagon* step **5**; then join the hearts as in *Triple hexagon* step **4**. Make hanger and finish as for *Long hexagon* steps **6-7**.

Full-size traceable templates

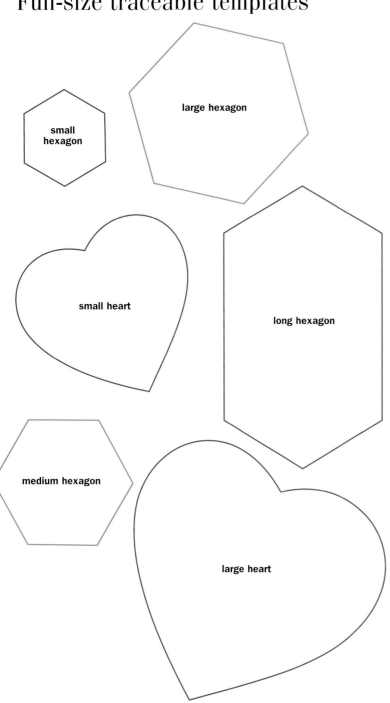

small hexagon

large hexagon

small heart

long hexagon

medium hexagon

large heart

Stitch library
Glove stitch

This stitch creates a decorative edge when you join two pieces of fabric together.

1 Working the foundation stitch Take a small upward stitch through both layers of fabric, close to the edges. Re-insert needle upwards through the same holes; pull up the thread to form another stitch. Neaten the thread end by tucking it out of sight between the two fabric layers.

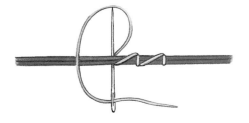

2 Working next stitches Take the needle to the left, slanting the thread over the fabric edges. Repeat step **1** to form the next foundation stitch.

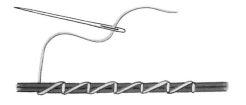

3 Continuing stitching Continue taking the needle to the left, slanting the thread over the fabric edges and repeating step **1** to form each foundation stitch. Complete the row with a foundation stitch, hiding the thread end in between the fabric layers.

Star-spangled specs case

*Diamond eyelets in floss and metal thread sparkle like stars
against a night sky of brilliant blue tent stitch worked
with fine crewel wool.*

Tent stitch, or needlepoint, is one of the most enduringly popular of all canvaswork stitches – and rightly so. Not only is it simple to work, but it also covers beautifully to create a thick, durable finish. Here it is combined with stem stitch and diamond eyelets in a simple but stunning pattern for a spectacles case.

The diamond eyelets are basically straight stitches radiating from a central point. In this instance, they are worked in squares of six canvas threads with embroidery floss and gold thread. You could change the thread colors to make silver stars instead, if you prefer, or use up odds and ends of thread to make multi-colored stars.

When using the gold thread, work with short lengths of 20cm (8in) or so to reduce the likelihood of it fraying, snagging or knotting.

▲ *This fabulous spectacles case of sparkling gold and deep blue makes a wonderful present. We have stitched the back but to save time you could use fabric – tweed would match the speckled effect.*

Stitch library
Diamond eyelets

This pretty stitch is often used for details, such as the eye of a bird or the center of a flower. Here it is worked over six canvas threads, but it can also be worked over eight. It takes a little practise to work this stitch smoothly, so make a few test stitches on scrap canvas first.

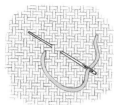

1 Bring the needle up three threads to the left of the center hole. Take it down in the center hole, then up one hole above and to the right of the starting point.

2 Work clockwise around the hole as shown, always taking the needle down in the center and bringing it up at the edges, until the eyelet is complete.

Making the spectacles case

This is worked in basketweave tent stitch (see page 70) and diamond eyelets. For the darker squares of tent stitch and the back of the case, use one strand of each shade of blue wool for a tweed effect. The paler squares are one color.

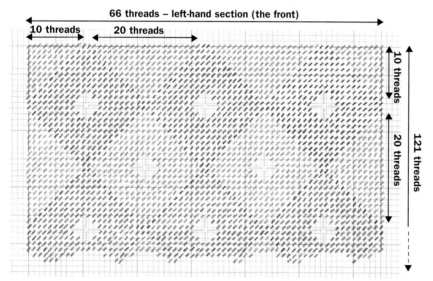

66 threads – left-hand section (the front)

10 threads

20 threads

10 threads

20 threads

121 threads

1 **Getting started** Bind canvas edges with masking tape, then mark a rectangle 132 threads wide by 121. Mark the vertical center. On the left-hand section (the front), outline the pattern in tent stitch. Using one strand of floss and the smaller tapestry needle, work four stitches to mark each eyelet position.

2 **Filling in the pattern** Start at upper right corner. Fill in pattern in basketweave tent stitch (see page 70), using 566 for light squares and one strand each of 566 and 928 for dark squares. Work back of case in solid tent stitch, as for dark squares. Work the diamond eyelets using four strands of 3822 and one of Fil or mi-fin. Block the canvas to re-shape it.

3 **Outlining the squares (optional)** Mount the work in a frame, then use six strands of 3750 and the chenille needle to outline the squares with stem stitch.

4 **Mitering the corners** Trim the canvas to within 11 threads of the embroidery. Steam press the turning to the wrong side on the top edge; repeat for the sides and lower edges but leave a single thread visible. Press the corners diagonally, then trim them to within three threads of the embroidery. Form miters and stitch them together, as shown. Glue the folded edges and leave to set under heavy books. (Place a sheet of plastic over the canvas to prevent the glue sticking to the books.)

You will need

- 28 x 28cm (11 x 11in) 18 mesh single-thread canvas
- Tapestry needles, sizes 20 and 22; chenille needle, size 20
- Appleton's crewel wools – six skeins (one hank) of 566 and four skeins of 928
- DMC floss – one skein of 3822; one skein of 3750; one reel of DMC Fil or mi-fin
- Lining fabric 20 x 19cm (8 x 7½in), lightweight, firmly woven
- Sewing thread to match lining; quilting thread
- Fabric glue
- Masking tape
- Slate frame (optional)
- Large press stud or Velcro dot

5 **Joining the edges** Using the quilting thread and smaller tapestry needle, whipstitch the canvas edges together from the bottom upwards, covering the raw canvas edges. Work several stitches at the corners for strength.

6 **Adding the lining** Press under and stitch a 2cm (¾in) hem on one shorter side of the lining. Fold the lining in half, right sides facing, so the hem is folded at the top. Zigzag stitch the raw edges together so the lining will fit in the case. Trim the fabric close to the stitching. Sew a press stud or Velcro dot to the upper, hemmed edges of the lining. Slip the lining into the case, matching the seams and the fastenings. Whipstitch the lining to the case along the top edges with strong thread.

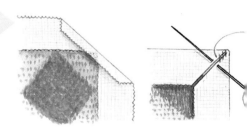

Canvaswork cushion

*A textured geometric pattern of square blocks, stitched
in a mosaic of festive colors, makes an eye-catching
Christmas cushion cover.*

A single canvaswork stitch can produce a result that is every bit as exciting as a combination of different stitches. Cushion stitch uses diagonal satin stitch to produce a regular pattern of square blocks. Changing the direction of the stitches adds to the textural effect as the embroidery catches the light, and the clever use of strong colors creates an attractive patchwork effect. The cushion cover shown above is worked in cushion stitch. The blocks are placed close together, and are outlined here with simple backstitch.

Like most crafts, some special materials are required for canvaswork (see page 70). Both the canvas and wool are sold by fabric and craft stores.

▲ *Blocks of cushion stitch are outlined with a grid of backstitch for a dramatic visual effect, reminiscent of stained glass. Use crewel wool for a fine outline or tapestry wool for a bolder effect.*

Using a frame

Although not essential, a frame helps to prevent the canvas being pulled out of shape. Hand-held frames come in a variety of sizes. Slate frames have adjustable sides and come in several widths. A rotating frame allows you to work on long pieces of work that are wound on as you progress.

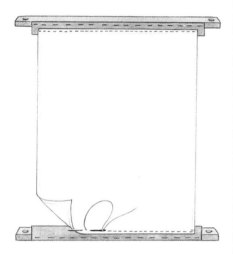

1 Attaching the canvas to webbing
Turn under 1.5cm (⅝in) all around the canvas and tack the turnings to hold them in place. Using button thread and backstitch, stitch the top and bottom edges of the canvas to the webbing on the rods, matching the center of the canvas edges to the center of the webbing.

2 Lacing the sides Insert the side rods to assemble the frame. Adjust the tension so that the canvas is taut. Using button thread, lace the sides of the canvas to the sides of the frame, leaving a length of thread at the top and bottom. Tighten the lacing from the center outwards, and knot the thread ends around the frame.

Stitch library

Cushion stitch

The blocks of diagonal satin stitches can be worked in the same or in different directions and colors to create a variety of geometric patterns. You can outline the blocks in backstitch using the same weight or a more lightweight thread.

1 Stitching the blocks For each block, work seven diagonal stitches over one, then two, three, four, three, two, and finally, one canvas thread intersections.

2 Working the outline Work a backstitch outline around each block, working each stitch over one canvas thread intersection.

Scottish stitch

The blocks of diagonal satin stitches can all be worked in one direction; alternatively, you can achieve a range of different visual effects by changing the direction of the stitches in each block.

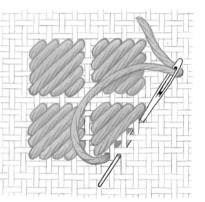

1 Stitching the blocks Stitch the blocks as described for *Cushion stitch* step **1** (left), but leave one canvas thread between each block of diagonal stitches.

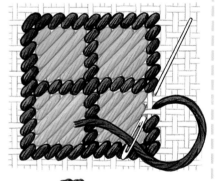

2 Outlining Outline the blocks with tent stitch, worked over one intersection of canvas (see page 70 for working tent stitch).

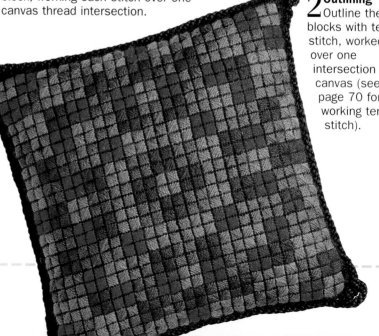

Making a cushion cover

Five glowing colors are used to work the stitch blocks, which are enhanced by a backstitch outline worked in fine black crewel wool. The finished cushion measures 26cm (10¼in) square.

You will need

- ◆ 48cm (19in) square of 10 mesh interlock canvas
- ◆ Dark tacking thread
- ◆ DMC tapestry wools – see chart for colors/quantities
- ◆ Two skeins black crewel wool
- ◆ Tapestry needle, size 20
- ◆ Slate frame and button thread (optional)
- ◆ 30cm (³⁄₈yd) of black furnishing fabric for back
- ◆ Black thread and pins
- ◆ 1.6m (1³⁄₄yd) of black cord
- ◆ Cushion pad, 30cm (12in) square

1 Preparing the canvas Cut canvas to size, allowing at least 5-8cm (2-3in) around the area to be worked. Mark the center with tacked lines, joining the center points of each side. Mount the canvas in the frame, if used, as in *Using a frame* on page 68.

2 Stitching the design Follow the chart, right, for color placement and stitch direction, and the *Stitch library*, left, as a guide to the stitches. Complete one half, then turn the chart round to work the second half, omitting the center two blocks of stitches. Outline blocks in backstitch using a double thickness of crewel wool.

3 Pressing Take the canvas off the frame. Place the work face down on a clean towel and press lightly with a steam iron. Leave to dry.

4 Making up the cover Trim canvas, leaving 1.5cm (⁵⁄₈in) all around the stitched area for seam allowances. *From backing fabric:* cut two 29 x 20cm (11½ x 8in) rectangles. Stitch the back of the cushion as on page 70. Using small hidden stitches, attach cord around the seamline; insert pad.

Chart

center blocks

KEY

7798 3 skeins	7666 3 skeins	7342 3 skeins	7690 3 skeins	7930 2 skeins

Materials and equipment

Canvas: This is available in a variety of mesh counts, determined by the number of holes to 2.5cm (1in). The higher the mesh count, the finer the canvas. A mesh size 12 is ideal for working with tapestry wool in tent stitch.
• **double thread** (Penelope) canvas is woven with pairs of threads. Small stitches can be worked over one thread, or larger stitches over both.
• **single thread** (mono) canvas has single threads giving holes of equal size.
• **interlock canvas** is the easiest type to work on. This is a mono canvas with threads which are fused together where they intersect, to create a smooth, immovable grid which does not distort when stitched. It does not fray when cut and can be worked without a frame.

When cutting out, allow a margin of 7.5cm (3in) around the finished piece.

Threads: Wool is the most popular choice of thread for canvaswork.
• **crewel wool** is a divisible 2ply yarn ideal for use on fine canvas. Use several strands together for coarser canvas.
• **tapestry wool** is a non-divisible 4ply wool. A single strand will cover 10 or 12 mesh canvas well.
• **Persian wool** is a slightly thicker 3ply yarn. This too is divisible, making it suitable for use on different mesh sizes.

Whatever wool you choose to work with, do not use lengths of more than 50cm (19¾in). Threads that are too long will fray and knot as you work.
Needles: Use blunt-ended tapestry needles. They are available in a range of sizes – the higher the number the smaller the needle. The eye must take the thread without it fraying, and the threaded needle must pass through the holes in the canvas easily without distorting them.

Stitching the back of the cushion

Turn in and machine stitch a narrow double hem down one long side of each of the two fabric panels. With the right sides together, pin the two back pieces to the cushion cover front, matching the outer edges and overlapping the two hemmed edges. Machine stitch as close to the edge of the embroidery as possible. Clip corners, turn right sides out and press lightly.

Stitch library

The three most commonly used canvaswork stitches are all forms of tent stitch. They are all worked over one canvaswork intersection to give short, slanting stitches and they look the same from the right side of the work. However, viewed from the back, you can see the difference and there are definite reasons for choosing to work in each particular stitch.

Basketweave stitch

Very useful for covering background areas, basketweave stitch is worked diagonally. The stitches change direction on the back of the work, so reducing the distortion of the canvas.

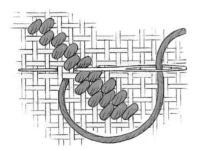

Working basketweave stitch
Work alternately up and down in diagonal rows, taking small stitches over one intersection of canvas until the area is filled.

Continental tent stitch

This method produces a long oblique stitch on the back, which gives a durable surface, suitable for cushions.

1 Working the first row Bring the needle through from the back of the canvas, leaving a 5cm (2in) thread end. Stitch from right to left as shown, working over the loose thread end to secure it.

2 Working the second row Work the second row of stitches below the first row, from left to right. Repeat these rows until the shape is filled.

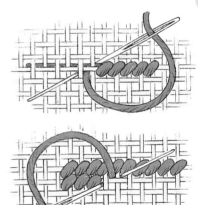

Half cross stitch

This forms small, straight stitches on the back. It uses less yarn, but produces a thinner fabric that is less durable.

1 Working the first row Bring the needle through to the front of the canvas, leaving a 5cm (2cm) thread end. Work from right to left, with the needle pointing upwards, stitching over the thread end.

2 Working the second row Work the second row from the left to the right, with the needle pointing downwards. Repeat these two rows to fill the shape.

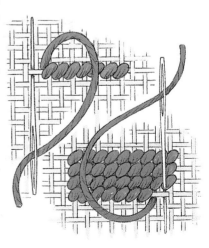

Fabric greetings cards

*These easy-to-make greetings cards are perfect
for all occasions and a great way to use up even the
smallest scraps of fabric and spare trimmings.*

Handmade cards are ideal for adding a really personal touch to special occasions, such as birthdays or anniversaries, or as unique greetings cards for friends and family. We all love to receive handmade gifts, so it really is worth taking a little extra time to make your own original cards.

These cards are a great way of using up any fabric left over from your soft furnishing or dressmaking projects – those pieces that are too small even for patchwork! Look out for unusual trimmings in fabric stores to embellish your designs, or raid your button jar and

sewing basket. You can use beads and buttons to highlight areas of a design, or scatter them randomly here and there as extra decoration. Beads are perfect to use as eyes for small figures and animals, such as for the teddy bear design, shown on page 72, while buttons or sparkling sequins provide a novel idea for other features.

Alternatively, if you want to keep things simple and make the cards from just fabric and thread, use decorative embroidery stitches to add the design details. Stem stitch is ideal for working flower stems, for example, while you

▲ *Handmade cards like these are very expensive, so why not make your own? It's a great way of using up left over fabrics, and odd buttons and beads.*

can outline motifs or highlight areas with tiny running stitches, and add textural interest with French knots.

Special presentation blank cards are available from fabric stores and craft shops. These come in a wide range of shapes and colors. Alternatively, it's easy to make your own card blank from lightweight card; just choose a color to suit your design.

Making a card

Each card is appliquéd on to a background fabric. The cards pictured have been made using a combination of checked, striped, plain and gingham fabrics, but you could substitute your favorite miniprints or floral fabrics – or just see what you have left over in your sewing basket.

You will need

- ◆ Fabric scraps – we used cotton/linen fabrics
- ◆ Lightweight card
- ◆ WonderUnder
- ◆ Assorted buttons
- ◆ Embroidery floss
- ◆ Craft adhesive
- ◆ Tracing paper and pencil
- ◆ Ruler
- ◆ Sharp scissors or a craft knife
- ◆ Needle

1 Preparing the card Using scissors or a craft knife, cut a 24 x 15cm (9½ x 6in) rectangle from lightweight card. For the fold, gently score down the center of the card with the blade.

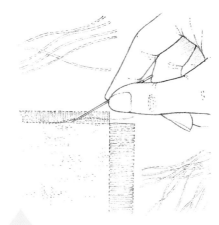

2 Preparing the background fabric Using the fabric weave as a guide for cutting straight lines, cut a 14 x 10cm (5½ x 4in) rectangle of your chosen fabric. To fringe the edges, use a needle to separate the threads along each edge; pull out enough to make a 1cm (³⁄₈in) fringe all around.

▼ *This fresh apple design is suitable for many occasions. The motif is defined by running stitch, with French knots as decoration. Dainty buttons add the finishing touch.*

3 Cutting out the inner rectangle For the apple, teddy bear, birthday cake and large heart designs, use pinking shears to cut out a second smaller rectangle, large enough to position the motifs on.

4 Preparing the motifs Choose which card design you want to make and trace the motifs on to WonderUnder. Roughly cut out, leaving a generous margin all around. Prepare each motif from chosen fabrics, as described on page 73.

5 Building up the design Working with one motif at a time and using the pictures as a guide to positioning, peel off the backing paper and lay each motif on the background fabric. Cover it with a damp cloth and press firmly with a medium-hot, dry iron. Leave to cool.

▼ *Children and adults alike will love this cute teddy bear, with his natty bowtie and buttons; his eyes are formed from two French knots. The motif suits a smaller card, so use a 10cm (4in) square of backing fabric, and make the card from a 24 x 12cm (9½ x 4¾in) rectangle.*

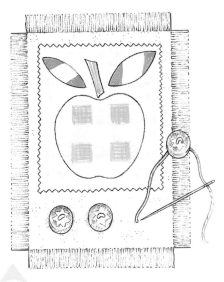

▶ *(Top to bottom) For a novel Christmas card, outline the tree with running stitches and highlight the star with tiny backstitches; French knots add the star's sparkle, while a green button makes the tree trunk. Embellish a heart design for a Valentines card with buttons; blanket stitch worked round the outline adds a dramatic finishing touch. 'Ice' a birthday cake with tiny French knots and decorate it with candles worked in satin stitch for a special birthday card.*

6 Adding trimmings Handstitch colorful beads and buttons to your card to highlight key areas of the design, as shown, or scatter them randomly as extra decoration.

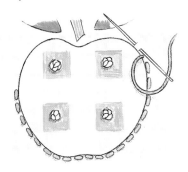

7 Adding decorative stitching Use simple embroidery stitches to enhance your design. Outline motifs with blanket stitch, backstitch or small running stitches. Use French knots and stem stitch to add details and textural interest.

8 Finishing off Attach the finished design to the front of your card using craft adhesive. You can still add extra stitching at this point, if you wish, working through all layers of fabric and the card.

▼ *On Mother's Day, why not say it with flowers? Use colorful buttons for the flower heads, then work the stems in stem stitch and decorate the plant pot with a few well-placed cross stitches.*

▼ *Show someone just how much you care with this enchanting hearts-theme card. For extra impact, mix contrasting fabrics with multicolored buttons and outline the individual hearts with tiny running stitches.*

Preparing motifs

Place the roughly cut out WonderUnder rough side down on the wrong side of the motif fabric and press with a medium-hot, dry iron to bond the materials together. With the right side of the fabric uppermost, use small sharp scissors to cut out the motif.

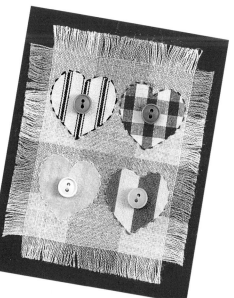

Trace diagrams

All but one of these motifs are the right size to fit a card that measures 15 x 12cm (6 x 4¾in). The exception is the bear, which is designed for a 12cm (4¾in) square card. Trace off the motif as a pattern and cut out each piece the number of times indicated.

Apple card

Stem Cut 1

Leaf Cut 1

Leaf Cut 1

Apple motif Cut 1

Leaf Cut 6

Valentines card

Large heart motif Cut 2 from different fabrics

Small heart Cut 1

Four hearts card

Heart motif Cut 4

Birthday cake card

Flames Cut 3

Candle-sticks

Top of cake Cut 1

Birthday cake motif Cut 1

(The candlesticks are embroidered in satin stitch)

Christmas tree card

Star Cut 1

Christmas tree motif Cut 1

Teddy bear card

Bear motif Cut 1

Bowtie Cut 1

Bowtie center Cut 1

Flower motif Cut 4

Flower pot card

Flower pot motif Cut 1

Pieced silk scarves

Every woman loves to receive a floaty summer scarf as a present. Shimmering satin and sheer chiffon are perfect partners for a light and dreamy look.

Scarves pieced together from two or three lightweight fabrics, or from a mixture of different colors of the same fabric, make a strong fashion statement and wonderful presents. These exquisite accessories are very expensive to buy in the shops, and it can also be difficult to find the exact color or shade you want. The perfect answer is to make one yourself. You can create the ultimate designer accessory for friends and family for a fraction of the price of a ready-made one, and you'll have total control over the color and style.

The scarves featured here are made of delicate chiffon and silk. In the blue checker-board version shown on the left, the almost opaque surface of the floaty chiffon is beautifully set off by the subtle sheen of the toning silk satin panels at each end.

For a strong statement, choose bright shades of blue and turquoise or green and jade. For a softer look, combine subdued shades of gently coordinating cream and gold or gray and pale blue. Alternatively, have fun with clashing poster-paint colors, such as bright orange, purple, red and clear yellow.

A simpler version of the pieced scarf, shown on page 76, uses just two fabrics. It has satin panels at the ends, but the central panels are cut as two single pieces. This style is very quick to make, yet still looks elegant.

◀ *Make a soft but bold statement with this pieced scarf in blue and turquoise chiffon. The silk satin panels at each end add weight, so the scarf drapes beautifully when tied.*

Making a pieced silk scarf

When you are making a pieced scarf, the key to success lies in the accurate cutting and stitching of the fabric shapes. Chiffon slips easily on a smooth surface, so to make it easier to cut the pieces accurately, withdraw threads from the fabric to provide a perfect cutting line.

Use pure silk chiffon, which will drape and hang beautifully. For the panels at each end, choose a lustrous lightweight silk satin in a toning shade.

The finished pieced scarf measures about 126 x 26cm (50 x 10½in). All the cutting measurements include 1cm (⅜in) seam allowances.

1 Cutting out *From chiffon:* from each color cut ten rectangles 20 x 15cm (8 x 6in). *From satin:* cut four rectangles, each measuring 28 x 20cm (11¼ x 8in).

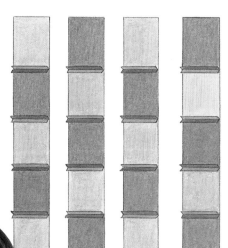

2 Stitching the chiffon Lay out the chiffon pieces, with short sides together, in four lines of five rectangles each, making sure the colors are placed correctly, as above. Pin, then stitch each line of rectangles. Trim seam allowances to 6mm (¼in) and press seams open.

3 Joining the pieces Taking 1cm (⅜in) seam allowances, stitch the rows of chiffon rectangles together in pairs to make two panels, checking the colors are placed in the correct order. Trim the seam allowances and press them open.

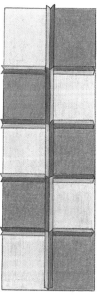

You will need

- ◆ Two x 40cm (½yd) of silk chiffon, 112cm (45in) wide, in different colors
- ◆ 30cm (⅜yd) of lightweight silk satin, 112cm (45in) wide
- ◆ Very fine dressmaking pins
- ◆ Matching silk sewing thread
- ◆ Knitting needle

4 Adding the satin panels With right sides together and 1cm (⅜in) seam allowances, stitch a satin rectangle to the short ends of each panel. Trim the seam allowances and press towards the satin.

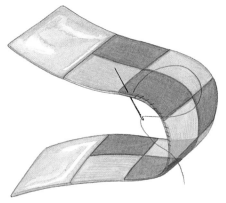

5 Finishing the scarf Place the scarf panels right sides together, matching the colors and seams. Taking 1cm (⅜in) seam allowances, pin then stitch all around the scarf, leaving a 10cm (4in) gap on one long side. Trim the seam allowances and turn through to the right side, carefully pushing out the corners with a knitting needle. Press. Slipstitch the opening with neat invisible stitches.

◀ *Using just two fabrics, this luxurious and subtle scarf teams a beautiful piece of printed silk with a toning plain shade. This scarf is longer than the checker-board version, so cut the two printed panels 116 x 28cm (45¾ x 11¼in). The end panels are the same size as before. Assemble the scarf following steps 4-5 above, taking 1cm (⅜in) seam allowances.*

Canvaswork accessories

*Richly colored patterns worked in simple tent stitch make
an eye-catching shoulder bag for daytime or evening. Wear it with
a matching belt for a colorful coordinated look.*

This dramatic bag is inspired by the rich embroidered textiles of Central Asia, whose creators have a natural affinity with hot, bold colors and intricate patterns. Small bags such as this are stitched by needleworkers to express their own creativity and are often masterpieces of design. Strong colors and fascinating patterns, many of them following tribal or regional traditions, combine to create exotic effects.

Tent stitch is perfect for working such designs, which rely not on surface texture, but on a combination of vibrant colors and complex patterns for dramatic effect. The bag is lined with black velvet for a soft and luxurious feel. For a final flourish, the lower edge is trimmed with tassels made from silky embroidery floss, just as the Asian needleworkers decorate their beautiful bags.

The finished bag measures 22 x 19cm (8¾ x 7½in) – which is just the right size for carrying a few necessities on an evening out. A bigger bag can be made by working the design on a 10 mesh canvas instead of the 12 mesh used here.

The border design on the bag has been used here to make a dramatic belt. Follow the colors given on the chart if you want to give the bag and belt as a matching set. Alternatively, use other shades if you are giving them as separate presents. You will need threads in four colors as well as black.

◀ *Take the vibrant designs of Central Asia as your inspiration for accessories like this canvaswork bag and matching belt. They are easy to make using simple tent stitch – the bold combination of pattern and color provides the impact.*

Bag chart

Key
DMC tapestry wools

Ecru	Black	7423	7740	7137
1 skein	3 skeins	3 skeins	2 skeins	3 skeins

Belt chart

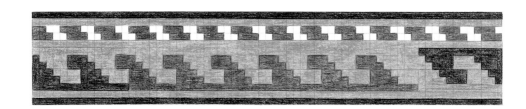

Making the bag

There's no need for a frame if you use the basketweave version of tent stitch (see page 70) – this method pulls the canvas in both directions, so distortion is minimal. For the strap, plait three strands of narrow cord together – this makes a flat cord which is easier to secure than thick, round cord.

You will need

◆ 35 x 30cm (13¾ x 12in) 12 mesh interlock canvas

◆ 30cm (⅜yd) black velvet

◆ DMC tapestry wools – see chart opposite for colors and quantities

◆ DMC pearl cotton – one skein each orange 971, red 815, beige 7423 and black

◆ Sewing threads to match pearl cottons, plus black thread

◆ 4m (4⅜yd) thin black cord

◆ Dark tacking thread and needle

◆ Tapestry needle, size 22

◆ Stiff white card

◆ Slate frame and button

1 Preparing the canvas To mark the center of the canvas, tack between the center points of opposite edges. Mount the canvas in the frame, if used, as on page 68.

2 Stitching the design Following the chart opposite, work the design in tent stitch, starting at the center and working outwards. Use the basketweave method of working tent stitch wherever possible (see page 70).

3 Pressing the work Take the canvas off the frame, and remove all tacking threads. Place the work face down on a soft towel and steam press lightly. If the canvas is slightly distorted, ease it into shape while it is still damp. Trim canvas to leave a 1cm (⅜in) seam allowance all around the embroidery.

4 Cutting out *For the bag back:* cut one 24 x 21cm (9½ x 8¼in) rectangle of black velvet. *For the bag lining:* cut one 46 x 21cm (18½ x 8¼in) rectangle of black velvet.

5 Stitching the bag With right sides together and taking a 1cm (⅜in) seam allowance, pin then tack the bag back to the canvaswork panel at sides and bottom. Machine stitch as close as possible to the edge of the embroidery. Trim seams, clip corners and press seams open. Turn to the right side and press lightly.

6 Making the strap Cut the cord into three. Hold the three ends together with sticky tape and plait. Secure the ends of the plait with sticky tape, then tack to right side of the bag at the side seams.

7 **Stitching the lining** With the right sides together, fold the lining rectangle in half widthways. Pin and stitch side seams, taking a 1cm (⅜in) seam allowance and leaving a 10cm (4in) gap in one side. Trim seams, clip corners and press seams open. Leave wrong side out.

8 **Finishing the bag** With right sides together, insert bag into lining. Pin and tack the top edges, matching the side seams. Stitch with a 1cm (⅜in) seam allowance, stitching as close to the edge of the embroidery as possible. Turn the bag right side out through gap in lining, and slipstitch the opening closed. Machine stitch close to the folded edge at the top of the bag.

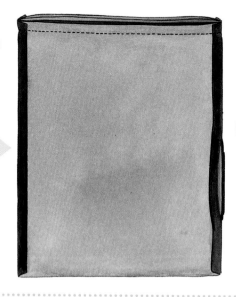

9 **Adding the tassels** Using pearl cotton, make three black, two red and two orange tassels, each 7.5cm (3in) long. Stitch them to the bottom edge of the bag, spacing them 2.5cm (1in) apart.

Making the canvaswork belt

The finished belt is 2.5cm (1in) wide and 87cm (34¼in) long. For a longer belt, cut longer pieces of canvas and petersham ribbon and work an extra pattern repeat – each pattern repeat adds an extra 9cm (3½in) to the finished length of the belt.

1 **Stitching the canvas** Referring to steps **1-3** on page 79, prepare the canvas and stitch it, following the belt chart; work five pattern repeats in each direction, varying the color combinations. At one end, work an extra 2.5cm (1in) in black. Press the work.

2 **Neatening the canvas** Trim the canvas to leave 1cm (⅜in) all round the embroidery. Leaving the end with the black stitching unfolded, fold the other three edges to the back along the edges of the stitching. Tack, making sure that no canvas shows from the right side. Press again.

You will need

- ◆ 100 x 12.5cm (40 x 5in) 12 mesh interlock canvas

- ◆ DMC tapestry wools – one skein orange 7740, two skeins each red 7137, beige 7423 and black

- ◆ 1m (1⅛yd) of 2.5cm (1in) wide black petersham ribbon

- ◆ Buckle 2.5cm (1in) wide with no pin

- ◆ Dark tacking thread

- ◆ Black sewing thread and needle

- ◆ Tapestry needle, size 22

- ◆ Small piece of black sew-on Velcro

3 **Adding the buckle** At the end with the black stitching, thread the belt over the buckle bar; fold to the back along the inner edge of the black stitching. Starting close to the buckle bar and picking up canvaswork stitches, not canvas, use black sewing thread to oversew the front and back of the belt together.

4 **Stitching the backing** Turn in 1cm (⅜in) at one end of the petersham ribbon. With the fold against the edge of the black stitching, pin it to the wrong side of the belt; turn under 1cm (⅜in) at the other end, trimming as necessary. Oversew all around, picking up the wool stitches and ribbon edges only. Remove tacking.

5 **Adding the fastening** The recipient should try on the belt so you can mark the positions for the Velcro fastening. Stitch in place.

▶ *The belt looks good teamed with the matching bag, or on its own with trousers and skirts.*

Embroidered brooches

Use very simple stitches to create these two bright and charming embroidered brooches. There's a little bumble bee and a pear motif, neatly framed inside narrow embroidered borders.

These two exquisite brooches are miniature works of art. They could be pinned to the collar of a jacket or on to a sweater, or added to brightly colored felt berets for a cheerful note of humor. On both brooches, the main motif shape is padded with felt before working the embroidery. This gives a slightly raised effect and makes the design stand out from the background. The brooches are given a final flourish with a narrow embroidered border.

These delightful brooches are worked with simple embroidery stitches, and require only basic sewing skills to create a special accessory and unique gift. Very small amounts of fabric and thread are needed, so they are inexpensive to make. Follow the color combinations shown here or, if you prefer, use odds and ends of threads from your sewing basket for your own version.

◄ *The fat and cheerful bumble bee brooch makes an amusing accessory on a bright yellow beret. Delicate stitching worked over padding brings a clever, three-dimensional look to the finished design. The detail of the brooches (see below) shows you the actual finished size of each design.*

Making the brooches

The motifs are brought to life with the addition of a little felt padding over the main shapes, giving a slightly raised, three-dimensional effect. A narrow embroidered border around the edge of each brooch completes the design and provides a neat frame.

You will need

For each brooch:

- 25cm (10in) square of lightweight unbleached calico, pre-washed

- Tracing paper, pen and masking tape

- Dressmaker's carbon paper

- 5cm (2in) squares of felt as follows: white felt for front and either navy blue for bee, or green for pear

- White sewing thread

- Embroidery hoop (optional)

- Crewel needle, size 7

- Anchor floss – one skein of each color on the key (see page 84) plus chosen color for pear motif border

- 2.5cm (1in) brooch bar (with holes)

Stab stitch

This is a useful technique for hand-stitching a thick fabric, where it would be difficult to form a whole stitch in one movement.

Working the stab stitch Simply take the needle through the fabric and pull the thread all the way through in one direction. Then repeat in the opposite direction.

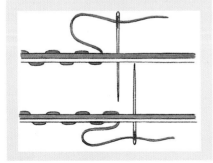

Making bumble bee brooch

1 Transferring the design Trace off the design (see page 84), including the outer edge lines. Place the tracing on the calico and secure it in place with masking tape. Slip the dress-maker's carbon paper under the tracing and draw over the lines of the design to transfer them to the calico. Mount the fabric in the hoop (optional).

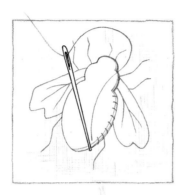

2 Padding the bee's body Trace the shape of the bee's body on to paper and cut it out. Use this as a template to cut out a body shape from the white felt. Place the white felt body in position on the calico. Using white sewing thread, stab stitch all round the felt body to secure it in place.

3 Stitching the background Using two strands of the background color 164 (see page 84), fill in the background of the brooch with long and short stitch, beginning at the top of the shape and working down and around the bee's body.

4 Stitching the legs and antennae Using two strands of dark gray 400, work the legs and antennae of the bee in stem stitch.

5 Stitching the wings Using two strands of white thread, fill in the wings with long and short stitch, worked in direction indicated on the stitching chart (page 84). Use a single strand of pale gray 399 over the top of the white to work the veins in stem stitch.

6 Stitching the body Using two strands of black, work black stripes on the body in satin stitch. Start with the head and work the stitches across the body shape. With two strands of the paler gold 307, work the stripe below the head in satin stitch. Work the second gold stripe with long and short stitch, changing from pale gold 307 to dark gold 308 as indicated on the stitching chart.

7 Cutting out the brooch Cut out the brooch, leaving a 1cm (³⁄₈in) border of fabric all around for turning under. Fold the turnings to the back of the brooch, leaving 2mm (¹⁄₁₆in) of calico all round the edge of the embroidery; finger press in place.

8 Stitching the border Overlapping background stitches slightly, and pushing needle through from back to front, stitch border in closely worked overcast stitch, to cover the calico edge. You can work overcast stitch in either direction: take small diagonal stitches over the edge, bringing the needle out to side of previous stitch. Here, they are worked very close together. Work blocks of black first, spaced evenly around the edge, then fill in the spaces with dark gold 308.

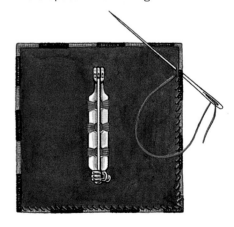

9 Finishing the brooch For the backing, cut a piece of navy blue felt the same size as the brooch. Stitch the brooch bar securely to the center of the felt with matching thread. Carefully pin the felt to the back of the embroidered brooch and stitch in place with small, neat overcast stitches, using the same matching thread.

Making pear brooch

1 **Transferring the design** Trace the design and transfer on to the calico, as in *Making bumble bee brooch* step **1**. Mount the fabric in the hoop.

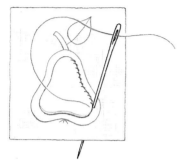

2 **Padding the pear** Trace off pear outline on to white paper. Cut out and use as a template to cut two pear shapes from white felt. Trim off 3mm (⅛in) all around the edge of one felt shape and place it in position on the calico; stab stitch all around to secure. Place larger felt pear shape on top and stab stitch to secure, as before.

3 **Stitching the background** Thread a single strand of each background color 239 and 257 in needle together. Then work the background in long and short stitch, starting at top and working down and around the pear motif.

4 **Stitching the stalk and leaf** Use a single strand throughout. Using brown 360, work stalk in long and short stitch, starting at the top and working down towards the pear. Use 253 to embroider the leaf in satin stitch in two halves, working stitches in direction shown on stitching chart. Use 269 to work leaf vein in stem stitch and base of pear in small, straight stitches.

5 **Stitching the pear** Using one strand each of orange, 303, 314 and 324, work pear in long and short stitch, starting at the top and working down. Follow stitching chart for changes of color. Using 269 and the picture as a guide to positioning, work speckles on the pear in small, vertical stitches.

6 **Finishing the brooch** Follow *Making bumble bee brooch* steps **7-9**, for cutting out the brooch, stitching the border, and finishing the brooch, only this time work the overcast border in a single color of your choice.

▶ *Here the luscious pear is framed with a border in red 46 to tone with a cheerful red beret.*

Traceable pattern

Stitching chart

KEY

Anchor floss

307		399	
308		white	
164		black	
400		▲ Stitch direction ▼ arrow	

▲ *This larger-than-life picture enables you to see the stitches used to work the brooches more clearly. Use a combination of the picture (above) and the stitching charts (left) as a guide to positioning the various colors and stitches.*

Traceable pattern

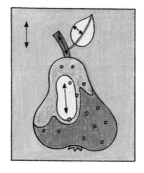

Stitching chart

KEY

Anchor floss

314		257	
303		253	
324		360	
239		269	▲ Stitch direction ▼ arrow

Grosgrain accessories

Take lengths of colorful grosgrain ribbon and turn them into stunning accessories for handbag or dressing table – try a glasses case, tissue holder, key ring, or even a zip-up purse.

Grosgrain ribbons take on a whole new look when they are cut into lengths and stitched together. The result is a strong, firm fabric with a subtle sheen and an interesting ribbed texture. Once you have practiced joining lengths of grosgrain ribbon together – stitching very close to the edge – it's easy to turn them into stylish handbag accessories, like those shown above.

Grosgrain ribbon comes in a range of colors. Choose a bright hue so the items will be easy to spot in the recesses of a bag, or a darker color for a more sophisticated look. If you can't find grosgrain, petersham is an excellent substitute. The insides of the cases are protected with mediumweight sew-in interfacing. For the optional chains use plug chain, from hardware stores.

▲ *Grosgrain ribbon – often used to decorate hats – is the perfect basic material for making these stylish accessories. There's a smart case to protect spectacles, a generously sized zip-up purse, a useful holder for tissues and a simple key ring.*

Making the glasses case

The finished glasses case measures about 18 x 7.5cm (7 x 3in), which is large enough to take most spectacles. If you want to make the case wider, cut extra pieces of grosgrain ribbon; to make it longer, cut longer ribbons.

You will need

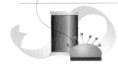

- 3.4m (3¾yd) of 15mm (⅝in) wide grosgrain ribbon

- 20cm (8in) square of sew-in interfacing

- Matching thread

- 70cm (¾yd) long chain and pincers (optional)

1 Cutting out *From grosgrain ribbon:* cut thirteen 25cm (10in) long strips for the case and one 12.5cm (5in) strip for the loop.

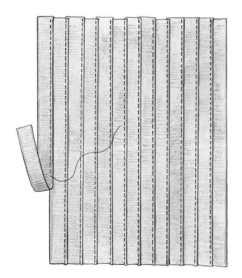

2 Joining the strips Lay two of the longer strips down on the work surface, overlapping them by 3mm (⅛in); tack in place. Keeping the overlaps facing the same way, repeat to join all the longer strips to make a piece approximately 16cm (6¼in) wide. Machine stitch the overlapped edges, remove the tacking and press.

▶ *The glasses case is a stylish way to protect spectacles or sunglasses from dust and damage. Add a neck chain if the recipient is always losing them!*

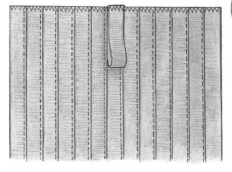

3 Adding the loop Trim the raw edges so that the piece measures 22cm (8¾in) deep. Fold the shorter strip in half to make a loop. With raw edges level, center the loop at the top edge and tack to hold in place. Zigzag stitch the raw edges, catching in the ends of the loop.

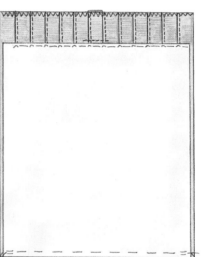

4 Adding the interfacing Trim the interfacing so it is 3cm (1¼in) shorter and 1.2cm (½in) narrower than the grosgrain. Center it on the grosgrain, with lower edges level; tack lower edges together. Secure top of interfacing with hand stitches, stitching through underlapping edges of ribbons, so that no stitches show on the right side. Machine stitch the loop to grosgrain just above the interfacing.

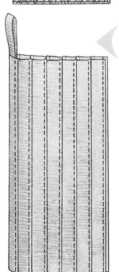

5 Forming case At the top edge, press 3cm (1¼in) to the wrong side and slipstitch to the interfacing. Then with right sides together, fold the case in half widthways. Stitch the lower edge, taking a 1cm (⅜in) seam allowance. Trim the interfacing from the seam allowance.

6 Finishing Turn the case right side out and match the edges of the grosgrain at one side; tack, then stitch. If you wish, thread the chain through the loop. Using pincers, open the link at one end, thread through the last link at the other end, then close the link to secure.

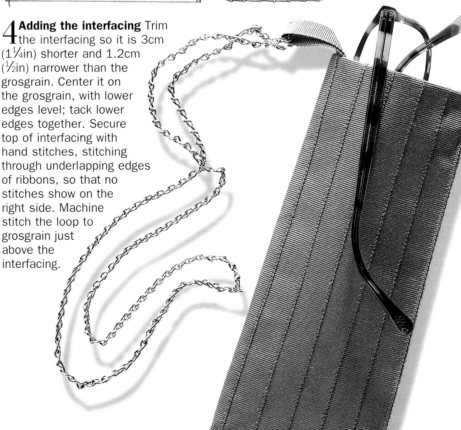

Making the tissue holder

The tissue holder measures 13 x 8cm (5⅛ x 3¼in) – just the right size for a mini pack of tissues. It is made in a similar way to the glasses case: you will need 3m (3¼yd) of 15mm (⅝in) wide grosgrain ribbon and 20 x 15cm (8 x 6in) of sew-in interfacing.

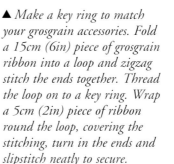

1 Cutting out *From grosgrain ribbon:* cut ten 25cm (10in) long strips for the holder and one 12cm (5in) long strip for the loop.

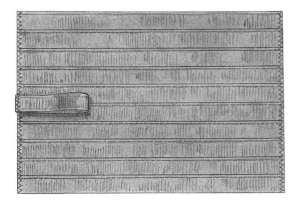

2 Joining the strips Following *Making the glasses case* step **2**, but with the strips arranged horizontally, join the longer grosgrain strips. Trim the raw ends so the piece measures 21cm (8¼in) across. Fold the loop strip in half. With raw edges level, tack the loop to the center of one short edge. Zigzag stitch the raw edges, catching in the ends of the loop.

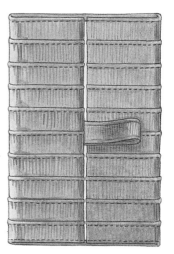

▲ *Make a key ring to match your grosgrain accessories. Fold a 15cm (6in) piece of grosgrain ribbon into a loop and zigzag stitch the ends together. Thread the loop on to a key ring. Wrap a 5cm (2in) piece of ribbon round the loop, covering the stitching, turn in the ends and slipstitch neatly to secure.*

ADDING A LINING

Tip

If you want to line your grosgrain glasses case, cut two pieces of lining fabric the same size as the case plus 1cm (⅜in) all round. With right sides together, stitch the lining pieces together around the side and lower edges. Then turn and press a 1cm (⅜in) hem at the top. With wrong sides together, slip the lining inside the item and slipstitch the pressed edge in place.

3 Adding interfacing Trim the interfacing so it is 3cm (1¼in) smaller lengthways and 1.2cm (½in) smaller widthways than the grosgrain. Center it on wrong side of grosgrain, and handstitch side edges in place, stitching through underlapping edges of the grosgrain so stitches do not show on the right side. Machine stitch the loop to the grosgrain, stitching level with edge of interfacing.

4 Neatening the edges On both side edges, turn 3cm (1¼in) to the wrong side and handstitch to the interfacing to secure.

5 Finishing the tissue holder Fold the holder, wrong sides together, so that the hemmed edges meet at the center and the top and bottom edges are neatly aligned. Tack, then machine stitch across the top and bottom edges to secure each end of the holder.

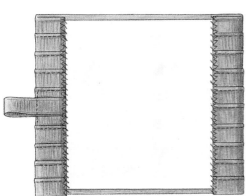

Making the purse

The finished zip-up purse measures about 15 x 12cm (6 x 4¾in). It makes a secure and convenient container for cash or make-up, and is just the right size to carry around in your handbag.

You will need

- 5.8m (6⅛yd) of 15mm (⅝in) wide grosgrain ribbon
- 15cm (6in) zipper
- 20 x 50cm (8 x 20in) of interfacing
- Scrap of stiff card
- Matching thread
- 60cm (24in) long chain and pincers (optional)

1 Cutting out *From grosgrain ribbon:* cut twenty-two 25cm (10in) strips for the purse and one 10cm (4in) strip for the loop.

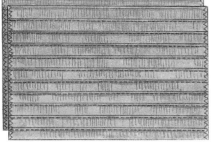

2 Joining the strips Following *Making the glasses case* step **2**, on page 86, but with the strips arranged horizontally, join the longer strips to make two separate pieces with eleven strips each. Trim the raw ends so each piece measures 21cm (8¼in) wide. Machine zigzag stitch the raw edges of both pieces.

▶ *With its generous gusset there's plenty of room in the zip-up purse for storing items such as lipsticks and eyeshadow palettes – or even a wad of banknotes!*

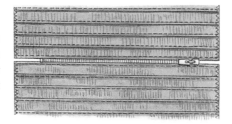

3 Adding the zipper Lay the pieces right side up, with the overlapping edges pointing to the center. Insert the zipper centrally, matching the grosgrain edges to outer edges of zipper teeth and positioning ends of zipper teeth equal distance from the grosgrain edges.

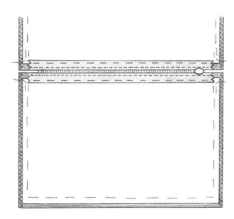

4 Adding the interfacing Cut two pieces of interfacing to fit the grosgrain pieces. With purse wrong side uppermost, tuck the top edge of a piece of interfacing under each edge of the zipper tape. Handstitch the tape to the interfacing with a running stitch. Tack interfacing to the grosgrain around remaining edges.

5 Stitching the seams Open the zipper. With right sides together, stitch the side and lower edges, taking a 1cm (⅜in) seam allowance and backstitching at seam ends. Trim interfacing from the seam allowances.

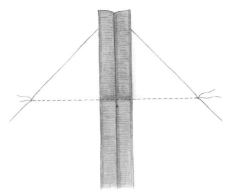

6 Shaping the bag At each lower corner, match the side and base seams, right sides together, and pin. Measure 4cm (1½in) from the corner and machine stitch across at right angles to the seam. Repeat to shape the corner at the bottom stop of the zipper, stitching across just below the stop. Then fold the loop strip in half, and shape the remaining corner as before, tucking the raw ends of the loop into the corner before stitching.

7 Finishing Cut a piece of stiff card to fit the base and slip in place. If you wish, add the chain, as shown in *Making the glasses case* step **6** on page 86.

Organza sachets

Delicate organza sachets of sweet-smelling potpourri make delightful gifts. The sheer fabric allows the natural shapes of the petals to show through and the scent to pervade.

Semi-transparent, crisp fabrics, such as organza and organdie, are the starting point for these fragile-looking, scented sachets. The sachets are made in a similar way to flanged cushion covers; the central square of stitching forms a flange of fabric which frames the potpourri and holds it in place. For a secure finish, the outer edges of the sachets are neatened with narrow French seams.

The sheer fabric lets the texture of the potpourri show hazily through – but it also exposes any uneven stitching! For a pleasing finish, take the time to stitch the sachets carefully. If you aren't happy with the result, you can always hide any imperfections around the edges with narrow satin ribbon. You may like to embellish the sachets with ribbon any-way, or add embroidery stitches, such as the French knots shown above.

▲ *Too good to hide away in a drawer, these luxurious sachets look and smell magnificent. To enhance the scent, add a few drops of essential oil to the potpourri before making up the sachets. The finished sachets could be displayed in a glass bowl on top of a shelf or chest of drawers; or stitch a fabric loop to one corner so they may be hung on a hook or hanger.*

Making the sachets

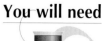

You will need

For each sachet:

◆ **Two 18cm (7in) squares of organza**

◆ **Needle and matching thread**

◆ **Potpourri**

◆ **Ribbon for trimming or embroidery floss for French knots (optional)**

1 Stitching edges Pin the squares together, with wrong sides facing. (*Note: if using organza, either side may be used as the right side.*) Stitch around three sides, 1cm (³⁄₈in) in from raw edges. Trim seam allowances on the stitched sides to 3mm (¹⁄₈in).

2 Finishing French seams Turn sachet wrong side out and press, with first row of stitching exactly at edge. Stitch around same three sides, 6mm (¹⁄₄in) in from outer edge, enclosing raw edges. Turn sachet right side out. Press, with second row of stitching at edge.

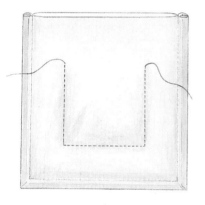

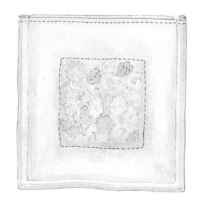

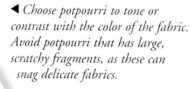
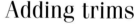

3 Stitching the central square Stitch three sides of sachet, 3cm (1¹⁄₈in) in from the seamed edges, starting and finishing 4.5cm (1³⁄₄in) in from unstitched edge. Fill sachet with potpourri, then tack along fourth side of central square.

4 Stitching the fourth side Stitch the fourth side of central square, to enclose the potpourri. Stitch the remaining raw edges of the sachet together, 6mm (¹⁄₄in) in from the outer edge. Trim the seam allowances to 3mm (¹⁄₈in).

◀ Choose potpourri to tone or contrast with the color of the fabric. Avoid potpourri that has large, scratchy fragments, as these can snag delicate fabrics.

5 Completing the sachet Separate the fabric layers below top stitched edge and push the seam down between the layers so that the seam and raw edges are enclosed. Arrange the newly formed folds of both layers level. Pin, then slipstitch, folded edges together.

Adding trims

Trimming with ribbon Beginning at one corner, pin ribbon around the sachet, level with the outer edge or inner stitching. Miter the ribbon to fit around three corners. On the final corner, tuck the raw end under and lap it over the first end. Tack then stitch in place near to both edges.

Stitching French knots Use six strands of embroidery floss. Starting at a corner, work a French knot. Pass the needle along on the inside of the seam, then bring it through ready for the next knot.

Cutwork butterfly mat

This delightful all-white mat is stitched on linen
using decorative cutwork techniques, tiny eyelets and surface
embroidery. It is edged with pretty cotton lace.

To make this beautiful cutwork butterfly tablemat, you first outline the design with running stitch and then with closely worked blanket stitch. Cutwork designs are specially created using two parallel lines so that certain areas can be cut away. In some cases bars, branched bars, picots and spiderwebs are added to fill the cut-away areas.

Here, overcast branched bars are used on the butterfly's wings but bars can be blanket stitched or woven depending on the type of design and weight of fabric used. Work all the bars at the same time as the outer row of running stitches, placing them in the middle of the two lines of stitching.

When you work the blanket stitch, it is important that you have the 'pearl'

▲ *This lacy mat is ideal for a dressing table where the feminine delicacy of its butterfly and floral motif may be appreciated to the full.*

edge facing those parts which will be cut away. This stitch gives the design a sharp outline and helps to prevent the fabric from fraying.

Full-size traceable template

Suitable fabrics

Light to mediumweight closely woven cottons and linens are best for cutwork embroidery as they keep their shape well when the background areas are cut away. You can use polyesters and poly-cottons but natural fibers will be softer to work with in the hand. When it comes to the embroidery, use a fine embroidery needle and choose either coton à broder or one or two strands of floss, depending on the weight of the fabric.

Making the mat

To make working on the cut-away sections easier, first snip the fabric. Then, working on the wrong side, pull the fabric towards the back of the stitching before snipping it away close to the stitching. Any little whiskers of fabric thread will be left on the underside, not at the edge of the cut-away section. The outer edge is trimmed with edging lace which has one scalloped and one straight edge. Choose one with a finished straight edge so it is neat on the wrong side.

1 Transferring the design Trace the design and add a 1.2cm (½in) seam allowance (as indicated by dashed line) to the oval given. Press the fabric to remove any creases. Place it on a flat work surface with the tracing on top and tape the top corners. Place the carbon paper, carbon side down, under the tracing and go over the design with a pencil. Trace the outer dashed oval line, which will be the cutting line.

You will need

- ◆ 46 x 33cm (18 x 13in) white linen
- ◆ One skein DMC white floss
- ◆ 122cm (48in) white lace trim, about 5cm (2in) wide
- ◆ Sharp, pointed embroidery scissors
- ◆ Embroidery needle
- ◆ 3mm knitting needle, or stiletto
- ◆ Dressmaker's carbon paper
- ◆ Tracing paper and pencil

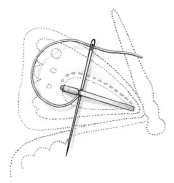

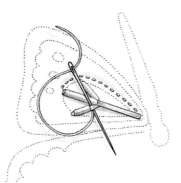

2 Making the center bars Using two strands of thread in the needle, outline the cut-away area on each wing around the outer line from the point to the top of the shape with running stitch. Then take the thread down to the inner point, make a small stitch and take it back to the top, securing it with another small stitch. Start overcasting down bar by wrapping thread around it.

3 Making branched bars Continue overcasting to about one third of the length of the bar. Take a stitch across to one side edge and a small stitch through the edge. Overcast back along this side branch to center bar. Make another side branch to opposite edge in same way and overcast back to center bar. Then complete overcasting down center bar. Finish outlining the outer line, then outline the inner line.

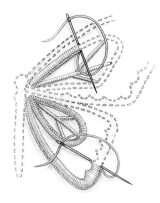

4 Outlining the butterfly Using one strand of thread, outline the butterfly with running stitch, including the body. Work blanket stitch over the two lines, placing the pearl edge of the stitch towards the cut areas on the inner wing decoration and to the outside edge on the outline.

▲ *Cut-away sections and eyelets combine with surface stitchery in this beautiful handstitched butterfly design.*

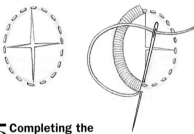

5 Completing the butterfly (Use two strands of thread for the remaining embroidery.) Embroider body and tops of antennae in satin stitch and stalks in backstitch. Work oval eyelets: first outline in running stitch as shown. Fold back snipped fabric and overcast. Trim excess fabric on wrong side.

7 The flowers and foliage Work the stems in stem stitch, the leaves in satin stitch and the flowers in blanket stitch, radiating the stitches so that they form a neat circle in the middle.

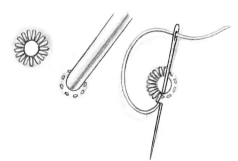

6 Working the small eyelets Begin by outlining one of the circles with running stitch. Pierce the center with the knitting needle or stiletto, making a small hole the size of the circle. Continuing with the same thread, overcast the edge, pulling the thread tight with each stitch and keeping your left thumb firmly over the circle so that it is not stretched out of shape. Fasten off at the back or bring out the needle ready to make the next eyelet.

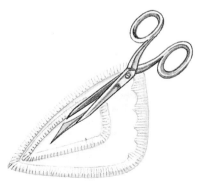

8 Cutting away background fabric Carefully working underneath the bar, make the initial cuts from the right side, snipping across the center and then outwards to any corners or to the outer edges. Turn to the wrong side and cut away the fabric close to the blanket stitch. Stroke any stubborn threads away from the edge and trim. Press on the wrong side.

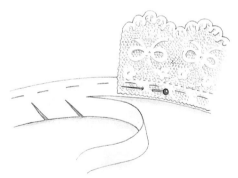

9 Adding the lace Cut out the mat and fold under a single 1.2cm (½in) turning, snip diagonally, tack 3mm (⅛in) from edge and press. Trim to 6mm (¼in). Position lace over the turning and pin in place, making small pleats or gathers so lace fits around the curved edges. Overlap the raw edges and handstitch one edge with zigzag stitch. Trim the overlap to 6mm (¼in), repeat on the second side. Using a single strand of thread and working from the right side, stitch the lace in place by hand with tiny running stitches, or by sewing machine. Remove tacking stitches and press on wrong side to finish.

Italian quilting

Create attractive relief patterns by trying out two forms of Italian quilting – corded and trapunto quilting. Unlike other methods, these involve padding selected areas only for striking textural effects.

W ith most quilting techniques you pad the entire item, giving extra body and warmth, but the Italian techniques of corded and trapunto quilting are purely decorative – only the motifs are padded while the rest remains flat.

The two techniques look completely different but they are created in much the same way. In both cases the main fabric is backed with a loose-weave fabric such as muslin. Then you stitch the design – by hand or machine – and finally insert the padding through holes made in the backing. What makes the two methods look so different is the

filling – soft cotton cord, thick knitting yarn or quilting wool for corded quilting and batting for trapunto quilting.

The two techniques can be easily combined in the same design because they are worked in such a similar way. For example, you could create a floral motif, using the trapunto technique to pad the flowers and leaves and corded quilting for the stems and tendrils. However, the techniques also work well on their own, as these cushions show, and it is probably easier to work them individually like this when you are trying them out for the first time.

You can use any close, even-weave

▲ *These cushions show two different approaches to quilting the same design. Corded quilting, used for the cushion on the left, creates a raised outline, while trapunto quilting gives the cushion on the right a softer padded look.*

fabric for these quilting techniques, but cotton and linen union fabrics are probably the easiest to work with. Choose a plain fabric if you wish to use a template or make up your own design. Alternatively, try using a patterned fabric – you can create some excellent results by quilting around the printed motifs.

Making the corded cushion

This cushion is 55cm (21½in) square but you can easily adapt the design to make the cushion a different size. The channels are outlined with running stitches done by hand but for speed you can use a long machine stitch, working carefully to ensure that your stitching lines are neat. If you wish, you can pipe the edges of the cushion.

You will need

- Tracing paper and pencil
- 57cm (22½in) square sheet of paper
- Dressmaker's carbon paper
- 57cm (22½in) square of plain cotton fabric
- Two 57 x 36cm (22½ x 14¼in) rectangles of matching cotton fabric
- 57cm (22½in) square of muslin
- 57cm (22½in) square of lining fabric
- Sewing needle and contrast thread or floss
- Tapestry needle
- Quilting wool, thick knitting yarn or prewashed soft cotton cord
- Quilting frame
- 55cm (21½in) square cushion pad

1 Tracing the design Fold the paper in half lengthways, then open it and fold it in half the other way. Unfold the paper which should now be divided by the foldlines into quarters. Using the template on page 98, trace it diagonally on to one quarter of the paper, with the curved end near the center of the paper and the circle pointing to one corner. Trace it again three more times on to the other quarters of the paper. Adjust the position of the tracings as necessary so they are symmetrical.

2 Transferring the design Use dressmaker's carbon paper to transfer the design from the paper to the right side of the cotton square. Make sure that the transferred design is made up of even channels about 6mm (¼in) wide.

3 Stitching the design Lay the fabric square right side up over the muslin and mount the two together in the frame. Starting anywhere you like, stitch the outlines of the channels in running stitch using contrast thread or two strands of embroidery floss. Begin with a backstitch to secure the thread. Keep the stitches as even as possible and avoid passing the thread between channels if it shows through the fabric.

4 Inserting the cord Thread the tapestry needle with a length of yarn or cord long enough to fill one channel with ease. Working with the muslin side uppermost, use the needle to force the muslin threads apart over one channel. Run the needle along the channel for about 3cm (1¼in) and bring it out on the muslin side. Don't pull the cord all the way through but leave a tail of 3mm (⅛in) instead of a knot at the beginning. Re-insert the needle and continue working in the same way along the channel.

5 Dealing with curves On tight curves, bring the needle out more regularly and make sure you don't pull the cord too tight or the fabric will pucker.

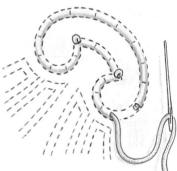

6 Dealing with angles Bring the needle out at the point of corners and acute angles. When you re-insert the needle and pull the cord through, leave a little loop of cord outside the channel for ease.

7 Finishing the cording When you have filled the whole channel, bring the needle out and trim the cord, leaving a 3mm (⅛in) thread end instead of making a knot. The cord is unlikely to slip out. Repeat the process to cord the remaining channels.

8 Assembling the cushion Complete the cushion as described in *Assembling the cushions* on page 97.

Making the trapunto cushion

The cushions in the picture on page 95 were made by quilting around the fabric motif, but you can copy the effect by stencilling the design using the instructions here. If you prefer, work the stitching lines on plain, undecorated fabric, or buy a fabric with a pattern that you like and stitch around its design lines. Make sure that the design lines join up to form small 'islands' which you can pad.

You will need

- ◆ Tracing paper and pencil
- ◆ 57cm (22½in) square sheet of thick paper
- ◆ Stencil brush and fabric paint
- ◆ 57cm (22½in) square of plain cotton fabric
- ◆ Two 57 x 36cm (22½ x 14¼in) rectangles of matching cotton fabric
- ◆ 57cm (22½in) square of muslin
- ◆ 57cm (22½in) square of lining fabric
- ◆ Needle and matching thread
- ◆ Tapestry needle
- ◆ Crochet hook (optional)
- ◆ Small, sharp scissors
- ◆ Toy stuffing or Kapok
- ◆ 55cm (21½in) square cushion pad

1 Making the stencil Make a paper pattern following step **1** on page 96. Carefully cut out the design around the outer edges of the cording channels using the small scissors. This is your stencil.

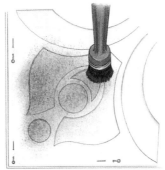

2 Stencilling the design Pin the paper stencil to the cotton fabric square. Dip the stencilling brush in the fabric paint, blot off the excess on scrap paper and then dab the brush on to the fabric, stippling on the paint. Don't be tempted to rush the job by loading the brush with paint – you'll end up with an uneven effect. Remove the paper stencil and iron the fabric to fix the paint, if required (see the instructions that come with the paint).

3 Stitching the design Pin the muslin square to the back of the fabric and machine stitch around all the design lines to create little stitched 'islands'. If you prefer, you can sew the motif by hand, using running stitch or backstitch.

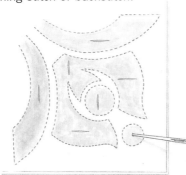

4 Making the openings Turn the fabric over and make a small slit in the muslin in the center of each stitched shape, following the fabric grain. You may need to make several small slits in large or complicated areas. For very small shapes, such as the corner circles, you can make a hole by pushing the muslin threads aside with a tapestry needle.

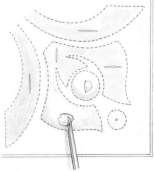

5 Padding the shapes Tease apart some filling material to remove any lumps and slip it into the slits in the muslin a little at a time. Use a crochet hook or tapestry needle to insert the padding and distribute it evenly. Turn the fabric over to check the effect on the right side and adjust the filling as necessary.

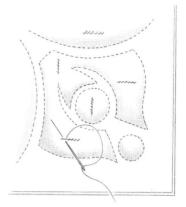

6 Securing the openings When you have finished padding a shape, bring the raw edges of the slit(s) in the muslin together and oversew them. If you have pushed the muslin threads aside to make a hole, ease them back together, using a tapestry needle to help you.

7 Making the cushion Complete the cushion as in *Assembling the cushions* below.

Assembling the cushions

1 Preparing the pieces Tack the lining square to the muslin side of the corded fabric to protect it. Pin, then stitch a double 2.5cm (1in) hem along one long edge of each cotton rectangle. Press the hems.

2 Stitching the seams Lay the corded fabric right side up and place the fabric rectangles right side down on top so that their hemmed edges overlap in the middle and their raw edges match the edges of the square. Pin, then stitch the layers together round the edges, taking a 1cm (⅜in) seam allowance. Remove the tacking, neaten the seam allowances and trim them at the corners. Turn the cushion cover right sides out and insert the cushion pad.

Full-size
traceable pattern

Introducing heirloom techniques

*As the name suggests, heirloom techniques turn
a simple cotton garment into a unique item of clothing
worthy of handing down over the generations.*

Heirloom techniques consist of sewing strips of lace and trims together to make a delicate and intricate fabric. You can place these strips either horizontally or vertically on the garment piece and vary them in width as you wish. You can further embellish the fabric strips with machine embroidery, pin tucks or hemstitching, or gather them to make ruched strips. You then cut this fabric to shape and make it up as part of a garment. Alternatively, use the fabric for a boudoir cushion.

The various heirloom techniques can be used to decorate areas of a blouse such as the yoke, collar, front and hemlines. The best styles of blouse to choose are those with few darts and side seams.

Cotton batiste and cotton lawn are ideal fabrics though they do tend to crease. Batistes and lawns made from a polyester and cotton mix are more crease resistant but are not so attractive. Lace trims made of pure cotton or mixtures with a large percentage of cotton feel soft and are easy to handle.

▲ *Heirloom strips are made by embellishing strips of fabric with decorative machine embroidery, pin tucks and ruching.*

You can also use insertion or edging lace. Slotted lace, which has double-faced satin ribbon woven through the slots, adds special detailing.

Entredeux is a trim that resembles hemstitching with seam allowances on both sides. It is stitched between strips of fabric and lace to make a strong and decorative join.

Making heirloom strips

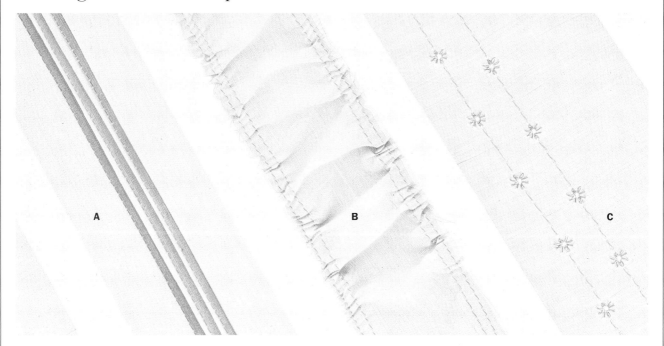

Cut or tear strips on straight grain of fabric – seams are less likely to pucker when cut across the width of the fabric rather than down the length. Cut each strip 1.2cm (½in) wider than the desired finished width to allow for seams. Allow additional width for pin tucks, too.

Cut the ruching strips 1½ times longer than the pattern piece to allow for gathering. Cut the other strips 2.5cm (1in) longer than the pattern piece. Apply spray starch to all strips except the ruching ones to make the fabric easier to handle. Spray starch on to the wrong side and press from the right side to prevent scorching.

Press, but do not starch, the ruching strips. After stitching it is best not to press the ruched strips as this might flatten their texture. Decorate fabric strips with pin tucks (**A**), ruching (**B**) as described on page 101, or use machine embroidery (**C**).

Designing an heirloom strip panel

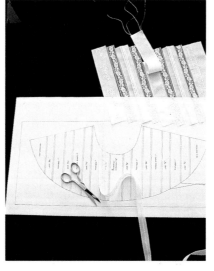

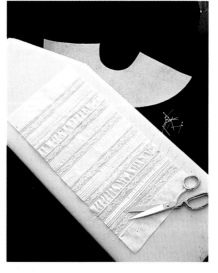

1 Making the pattern Make a full-sized pattern piece in tissue; trace on to firm paper. Plan the design using fabric strips and lace with entredeux placed between all joins. Place fabric strips at ends if edges are curved.

2 Cutting strips Measure pattern at its widest and longest points. Embellish and cut strips. The finished length of the strips should be 2.5cm (1in) longer than pattern.

3 Stitching strips Stitch entredeux, fabric strips and lace trims together (see pages 103–105) to form a rectangle or square. Press, avoiding ruched strips, and cut out to pattern shape.

Preparing fabric strips

Cutting pure cotton To straighten the end of the fabric, clip selvedge and pull a thread across to other selvedge. Cut on the pulled thread line. Clip again and pull a thread at desired width of each fabric strip; cut on pulled thread line.

Cutting cotton/polyester Clip selvedge and tear across fabric to straighten end. Clip again and tear at desired width of each fabric strip; press flat. Trim torn edges if desired, using rotary cutter and ruler.

Sewing ruched strips

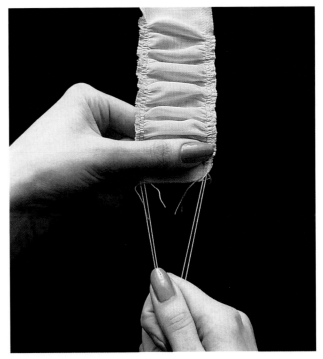

1 Working longest stitching Loosen needle thread tension very slightly. Stitch two rows of gathering thread on each long edge of strip with rows 3mm (⅛in) and a scant 6mm (¼in) from edge.

2 Ruching strips Holding all four bobbin threads together, pull up threads on each side of fabric to gather strip evenly to desired length. Knot gathering thread at each end.

Alternative ruching method

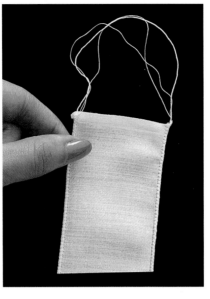

1 **Stitching first edge** Cut fabric and set stitch length and width (below). Place a thread along edge on right side of fabric, leaving a 7.5cm (3in) thread tail. Zigzag stitch over thread and the fabric will roll over the thread.

2 **Stitching second edge** Complete zigzag stitching along one edge. Turn fabric leaving a 10cm (4in) loop of thread before stitching down the other side. Leave a 7.5cm (3in) thread tail at the end.

3 **Ruching the strip** Pull both the encased threads from each end to gather both sides of the strip evenly. Gather to desired length and distribute gathers evenly. Knot gathered threads at each end.

Setting machine stitch length

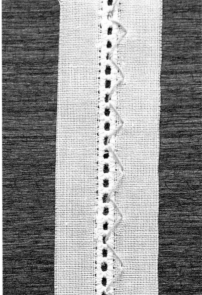

1 **Preparing for stitching** Cut a 10cm (4in) long strip of entredeux to use for establishing stitch length. Set machine for a zigzag stitch 3mm (⅛in) wide and for a length of 12-16 stitches per 2.5cm (1in).

2 **Testing stitch width** Stitch so the swing of the needle stitches into the hole of the entredeux at one side and into the fabric seam allowance at the other side.

3 **Setting stitch length** Adjust the stitch length so the needle stitches into each hole of the entredeux. Once this stitch length is established, it will remain the same for the entire project.

Joining heirloom strips

*Delicate heirloom strips are stitched
together with seams so fine that the finished
fabric looks like one piece.*

For machined heirloom sewing, stitch together fabric strips, laces and trims with narrow seams, which are neat and strong. A technique called rolling and whipping is often used. The seam allowances literally roll or curl and are secured with zigzag stitches.

When you roll or whip flat lace edging or insertion lace to a fabric strip, the extended material rolls over the lace edge. When you apply flat lace at a hem edge, you can press the rolled and whipped seam towards the fabric and topstitch through all layers.

Entredeux is a bought strip with embroidered holes along the center and a seam allowance along either side. The entredeux imitates the effect of traditional handstitched pulled-thread embroidery. It is often used between fabric and laces both to reinforce the seam and to make a decorative join. Slotted lace and entredeux can be further embellished by weaving narrow ribbon or embroidery thread through the holes in the trim.

Gathered lace often looks better than flat lace for trimming edges. Some laces are available with a gathering thread in place along one edge, or flat lace can be gathered by machine.

Setting machine stitch If you are using entredeux, cut a test strip and set the machine zigzag stitch to the correct length and width as described on page 102. The stitch should enter each hole.

Rolling and whipping

1 Arranging edges Place starched strip of fabric and flat lace, with right sides together and lace on top of fabric, so that the edge of fabric extends 3mm (⅛in) to the right of the lace.

2 Zigzag stitching Set zigzag stitch width so swing of left needle stitches on to edge of lace and right swing extends over the raw edge of fabric strip. As needle moves back to the left, the edge of the fabric strip rolls over the lace. If it does not roll, tighten needle thread tension. Press seam towards fabric.

Rolling and whipping entredeux

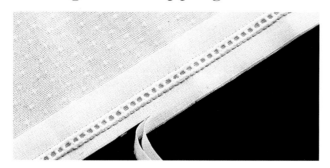

1 Stitching and trimming Trim seam allowance of entredeux to 6mm (¼in). Place starched strips of fabric and entredeux together with entredeux uppermost, right sides together and raw edges level. Straight stitch next to entredeux holes and trim the seam allowances to 3mm (⅛in).

2 Zigzag stitching Set zigzag stitch width so swing of left needle stitches next to the holes of entredeux and right swing extends over the raw edge. As needle moves back to the left, the edge of the fabric strip rolls. If it does not roll tighten needle thread tension. Press seam towards fabric.

Stitching entredeux to ruched strip

1 Stitching and trimming Trim seam allowance on entredeux to 6mm (¼in). Place ruched strip and entredeux with right sides together and raw edges level. Straight stitch next to entredeux holes and trim the seam allowances to 3mm (⅛in).

2 Zigzag stitching Set zigzag stitch width so left-hand swing of needle stitches next to the holes of entredeux and right swing extends over raw edge. As needle moves to left, edge of fabric strip rolls. If it does not, tighten needle thread tension. Press seam towards fabric using tip of iron so that ruching is not squashed.

Sewing flat lace together

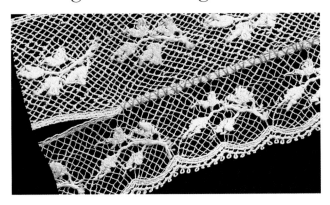

Butt edges of lace right sides up. Set stitch length as described on page 102. Stitch edges together using a narrow zigzag stitch.

Stitching lace to entredeux

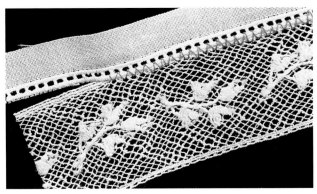

Trim away one seam allowance from entredeux. Butt trimmed edge of entredeux to edge of lace. Set stitch length, see page 102, and zigzag stitch along into entredeux holes.

Gathering lace to entredeux

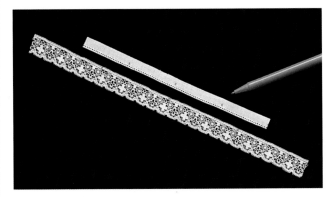

1 **Cutting strips** Cut entredeux 2.5cm (1in) longer than needed and trim away one seam allowance. Cut flat lace 1½ times longer than entredeux. Divide lace and entredeux into quarters and mark.

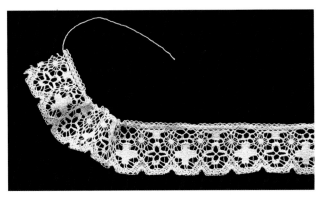

2a **Using lace with gathering thread** Pull the gathering thread on lace from both ends to gather the lace. Some laces have more than one thread in case one breaks. Match marks on lace and entredeux.

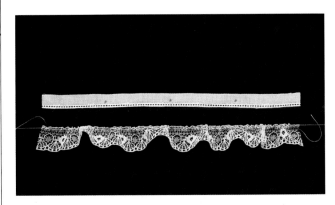

2b **Using lace without gathering thread** Stitch along lace edge using the longest machine straight stitch. Pull the bobbin thread to gather lace to fit. Match marks on lace and entredeux.

3 **Stitching together** Butt trimmed edge of entredeux to lace. Set the zigzag stitch length and width, see page 102. Stitch the butted edges together using a small screwdriver to guide the gathered edge. Remove gathering thread.

Cutting heirloom fabric

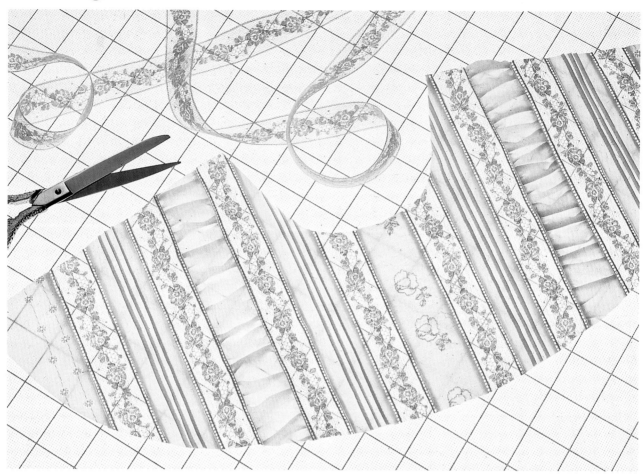

When you have joined all the strips together, block the fabric to set the shape before cutting out the pieces. Pin the fabric to a padded surface such as an ironing board so all the seams are straight. You may need to make some re-adjustments and re-pin for the best shape. Steam the fabric, taking great care not to flatten any ruched areas or machine embroidery. Allow the blocked fabric to cool and dry completely to set the shape. When cool, place the full-size pattern sheet on the fabric, matching the planned design as closely as possible.

Blocking and cutting

1 Pinning fabric Pin heirloom fabric to the padded surface so all the seams are straight. Use a straight ruler to check lines are straight, and adjust the pins if required.

2 Steaming fabric Hold a steam iron just above the fabric to steam set the shape. Be sure that you do not flatten ruched strips or machine embroidery. Allow to cool before removing pins.

3 Cutting out Position the pattern piece on the fabric with the pattern centered on the middle strip. The seams may not match the planned design exactly. Cut out piece to shape.

Heirloom christening robe

*Delicate heirloom techniques enable you
to make a christening robe so exquisite that it will be
treasured for generations to come.*

You can adapt most christening robe patterns to incorporate heirloom decoration into the design. A robe with a yoke is ideal. The whole front yoke can be made from heirloom fabric, as shown on pages 103–106. Puffed elasticated sleeves are also perfect for adapting to this type of decoration.

Most christening robe patterns have a long full skirt. If the skirt has vertical seams, you can put lace insertion in them with an entredeux trim either side. Most robes benefit from some additional decoration around the hem edge as this area is quite prominent when the baby is held.

To adapt a pattern for an heirloom band and frill, first cut off the required depth of frill and increase its width by 1½-2 times for gathering up. Then cut off the required depth of the band. Adjust all the skirt pieces in the same way.

If the robe is made from a fine fabric, a slip of opaque batiste prevents undergarments from showing through. On fine fabrics it is best to cut the front yoke double and adjust the back yokes so they are cut double with a fold at the center back.

The following pages show you how to achieve that ultimate heirloom look, together with some ways to adjust patterns and make accessories including the bonnet.

◀ *This robe has a pin-tucked frill at the lower edge and an heirloom-worked band around the skirt above the frill. The details show to particular advantage when the baby is held up for the baptism ceremony.*

Making an heirloom robe

1 Making yoke Cut front yoke from heirloom fabric, as on page 106. Cut yoke lining from the garment fabric. Tack front yokes together with right sides outside. Cut out two back yokes with the pattern's center back foldline on the fold of a double fabric layer. With back yokes still folded double, join them to front yokes at shoulder seams with French seams.

2 Sewing skirt band and frill Make band for skirt. Join entredeux to upper and lower edges of band. Adjust pattern for frill or cut frill according to pattern. Stitch the frill decoration, finish lower edge of frill with edging lace and gather top edge in same way as a ruched strip, as on page 101. Stitch frill to lower edge of band.

3 Attaching frill Join the skirt front and back at one side seam and center back seam. Stitch the band to lower edge of skirt. Stitch other side seam, matching frill and band seams. Gather the upper edge of skirt and stitch the skirt to the yoke.

4 Making sleeve Cut sleeve pattern along line marked for elastic; cut out sleeve in resulting two pieces. Cut slotted lace 5cm (2in) longer than circumference of arm. Gather both edges of sleeve as for ruched strips. Stitch to edges of insertion lace. Finish sleeve lower edge with edging lace. Stitch sleeve seam; set in sleeve. Thread ribbon through slotted lace and tie ends in bow.

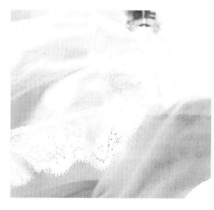

5 Trimming yoke seam Join entredeux to gathered lace. Trim entredeux seam allowance. Position entredeux on yoke next to seam with end folded under twice at edge of opening. Zigzag stitch in place to about 5cm (2in) from first corner.

6 Mitering trim Fold trim to a miter at corner so it just covers seam-line. Shape outer edge of lace at a right angle and overlap entredeux at inner corner. Miter other corners in same way. Continue zigzag stitching to 5cm (2in) from opening.

7 Finishing trim ends Cut trim to extend 1.2cm (½in) beyond edge of opening. Fold under 6mm (¼in) twice so trim is level with opening edge. Complete zigzag stitching. If wished, stitch entredeux with gathered lace attached round neck edges.

Making accessories

Making a ribbon rosette Cut 4.5m (5yd) of very narrow double faced ribbon. Beginning and finishing 30-35cm (12-14in) from each end, mark ribbon at 5cm (2in) intervals. Using double thread, handstitch through ribbon at each mark. Pull up tight and arrange loops. Knot thread ends. Handstitch rosette to garment.

Trimming a slip Trim neck and armhole seam allowances to 6mm (¼in). Make center back opening. Stitch both shoulder seams. Finish neck and armhole edges with entredeux joined to gathered lace. Finish ends in same way as page 108 step **7**. Stitch side seams. Finish hem edge with flat lace.

Finishing with French binding

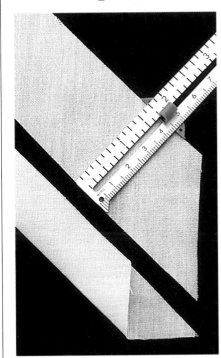

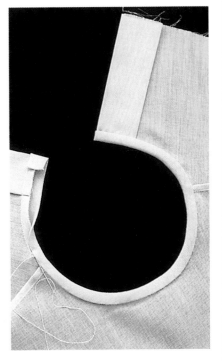

1 Preparing strips Cut a 4.5cm (1¾in) wide bias strip 2.5cm (1in) longer than the edge being finished. Press the strip in half lengthways with wrong sides together.

2 Stitching binding Trim garment along seamline. With raw edges level, stitch binding to right side of garment, taking 6mm (¼in) seam allowances. Wrap 1.2cm (½in) round to inside at each edge of opening.

3 Finishing binding Fold binding in half over the raw edge. Slipstitch the folded edge of binding to previous machine stitching on the inside.

Making the bonnet

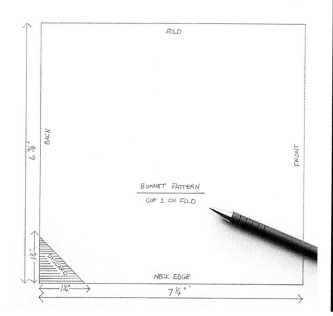

1 Making the pattern Draw a rectangle 18.5 x 17.5cm (7¼ by 6⅞in). Label the lower longer edge as neck edge and the top one as fold. Label side edges as front and center back. Mark 3cm (1¼in) in along center back and neck edge. Join marks with a diagonal line and discard the corner when cutting out.

2 Seaming back corner Join 38cm (15in) long heirloom strips to make fabric to fit pattern. End with slotted lace at center back edge and gathered lace at front edge. Fold fabric in half and, using pattern, trim lower edge and diagonal corner. Stitch diagonal edge with a French seam.

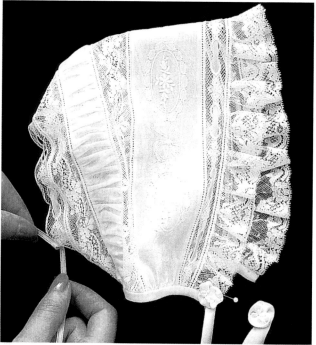

3 Binding neck edge Gather neck edge to 23cm (9in). Finish gathered edge with French binding, see page 109. Cut two strips of 1.2cm (½in) double-faced satin ribbon each 60cm (24in) long. Fold under 1.2cm (½in) at one end of each ribbon. Fold this end of ribbon in half lengthways and stitch 6mm (¼in) long running stitches along for 5-7.5cm (2-3in).

4 Finishing off Pull thread to gather ribbon up to form a rosebud. Stitch through back of rosebud to secure both the rosebud and thread. Handstitch rosebuds to front corner of bonnet's neck binding. Trim free ends of ribbon diagonally. Thread narrow ribbon through lace at center back. Tighten ribbon and tie in a bow to finish.

Baby booties

A pair of tiny booties adds the perfect finishing touch
to a baby's layette. Sew some exquisite booties as a special
gift to welcome the new arrival.

A ny of these baby booties would make an unusual christening present or a lovely gift to delight a new mom. The pattern is given in two sizes – to fit babies of 0–6 months and 6–12 months old. The booties are completely reversible and can be made in several different fabrics: make them in warm polar fleece for winter, in broderie anglaise or cotton poplin for summer, or in luxurious silk or brocade to match a christening robe.

Cut from a rich brocade or silk, and trimmed with expensive lace and pearl button fastenings, these booties are special enough to be treasured as a family heirloom. Whatever style you choose, you can be sure that your handiwork will be much admired and warmly received.

▲ *You can trim the upper edge of the booties with a pretty frill, made from gathered broderie anglaise edging or lace. Gather a short length of the same edging to make a rosette to decorate the toe of the bootie. A button finishes off the center of the rosette.*

Making the baby booties

You will need

For fleecy booties:

- 20cm (8in) of 90cm (36in) wide fleecy fabric
- 20cm (8in) of 90cm (36in) wide tartan brushed cotton for lining
- 1.2m (1⅜yd) red cord
- Ric Rac braid
- Matching sewing thread

For broderie anglaise booties:

- 20cm (8in) of 90cm (36in) wide broderie anglaise fabric
- 20cm (8in) of 90cm (36in) wide fine cotton for lining
- 1m (1¼yd) of 2.5cm (1in) wide broderie anglaise edging lace
- Four mother-of-pearl buttons
- Matching sewing thread

For brocade booties:

- 20cm (8in) of 90cm (36in) wide brocade
- 20cm (8in) of 90cm (36in) wide silk lining
- 1m (1¼yd) of 2.5cm (1in) wide gold lace
- Four pearl ball buttons
- Matching sewing thread

To make templates:

- Tracing paper and pencil
- Paper scissors

▶ *The fleecy booties are snug and warm for winter – for both indoor and outdoor wear. Rather than trimming them with a frill, try using Ric Rac or another type of narrow braid. Simply stitch the braid on by hand when the booties are complete, turning in the raw ends for a neat finish.*

All the pattern pieces include seam allowances of 6mm (¼in). Stitch the seams with right sides together unless stated otherwise.

1 Making the paper patterns Trace off the bootie templates on page 114. Cut them out.

2 Cutting out *From the outer fabric:* cut two uppers, two fronts and two soles. *From the lining fabric:* cut two uppers, two fronts and two soles. *For the brocade and broderie anglaise booties:* cut two bias strips of outer fabric 4 x 2.5cm (1½ x 1in). Transfer the dot markings to each bootie using tailor's tacks.

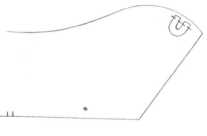

3 Making the fastening *For fleecy booties:* cut the cord into quarters and tack one end of each cord to the center front dot on the fleecy uppers. *For broderie anglaise and brocade booties:* fold bias strip lengthways in half and stitch along the long edge to make a button loop. Use a bodkin to turn strip right side out. With raw edges side by side, bend the strip into a loop and tack to center front dot on right-hand side of the bootie uppers.

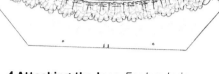

4 Attaching the lace *For broderie anglaise and brocade booties only:* cut two 26cm (10½in) lengths of lace. Cut the raw edges of both ends into a curve. Work a row of gathering stitches along the straight edge of the lace. Pin it to the fabric uppers between the center front dots. Pull up the gathers to fit and tack in place.

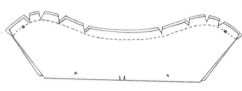

5 Bootie uppers With right sides facing, pin the fabric and lining uppers together. Stitch along the curved edge. Snip the seam allowance at the curves. Turn right side out, press and tack the raw edges together.

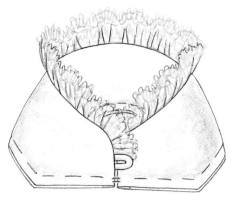

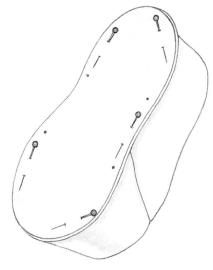

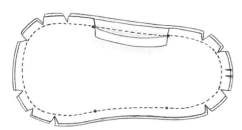

10 **Adding the sole linings** With right sides facing, tack the sole linings to the booties, matching dots and notches and sandwiching the booties between the outer sole and lining sole. Stitch sole seams. Snip seam allowance at curves and turn through. With the lining outside, slipstitch the lining opening closed.

6 **Stitching the bootie front** Butt the center front edges together and secure in place with a few stitches at the lower edges.

8 **Adding bootie soles** Turn the bootie through to the wrong side. With right sides together, pin the outer fabric soles to the booties, matching the dots and notches.

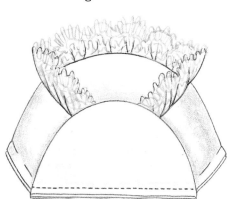

9 **Preparing sole linings** Snip to the dots on one edge of the sole linings. Press the seam allowance to the wrong side between snipped dots.

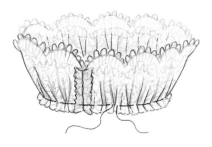

11 **Making the rosettes** Cut two 22cm (8¾in) lengths of lace. Stitch the ends together to make a ring. Work a gathering stitch along one edge. Pull up the gathers tightly and secure with a few stitches at the center. Stitch the rosettes to the fronts and stitch a pearl button at each center. For the fastening, stitch a pearl button on the left upper, under the button loop.

7 **Bootie fronts** Right sides together and matching the front edges, position a fabric front to a fabric upper and a lining front to a lining upper – the uppers are sandwiched between the two fronts. Pin, then stitch front seam. Turn fronts to right side and press the seam flat. Tack raw edges of fronts together.

▼ *These booties are for special occasions. You could achieve a similar effect using silk or satin – if you are making a christening gown, for example, you can use the off-cuts to make matching booties. For safety reasons, make sure that the buttons are stitched on firmly.*

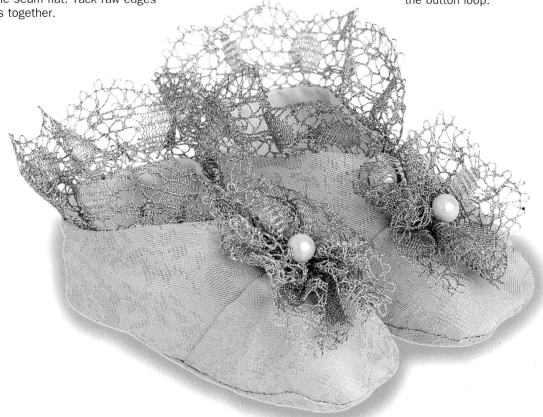

bootie sole
6–12 months old
cut 2 from fabric
cut 2 from lining

bootie sole
0–6 months old
cut 2 from fabric
cut 2 from lining

front edge

front edge

center front

center front

bootie front
0–6 months old
cut 2 from fabric
cut 2 from lining

front edge

front

bootie front
6–12 months old
cut 2 from fabric
cut 2 from lining

bootie upper
0–6 months old
cut 2 from fabric
cut 2 from lining

upper edge

upper edge

Tip

bootie upper
6–12 months old
cut 2 from fabric
cut 2 from lining

REVERSIBLE BOOTIES

To make the booties reversible, use two different
fabrics inside and out – red fleece on the outside
and tartan brushed cotton on the inside, for example, as shown
here. Use a tie fastening instead of a button loop and button,
otherwise you'll find that the loop is on the wrong side when
you turn the bootie through. You can still add trimmings but
make sure they are non-scratchy.

center front

center front

front edge

front edge

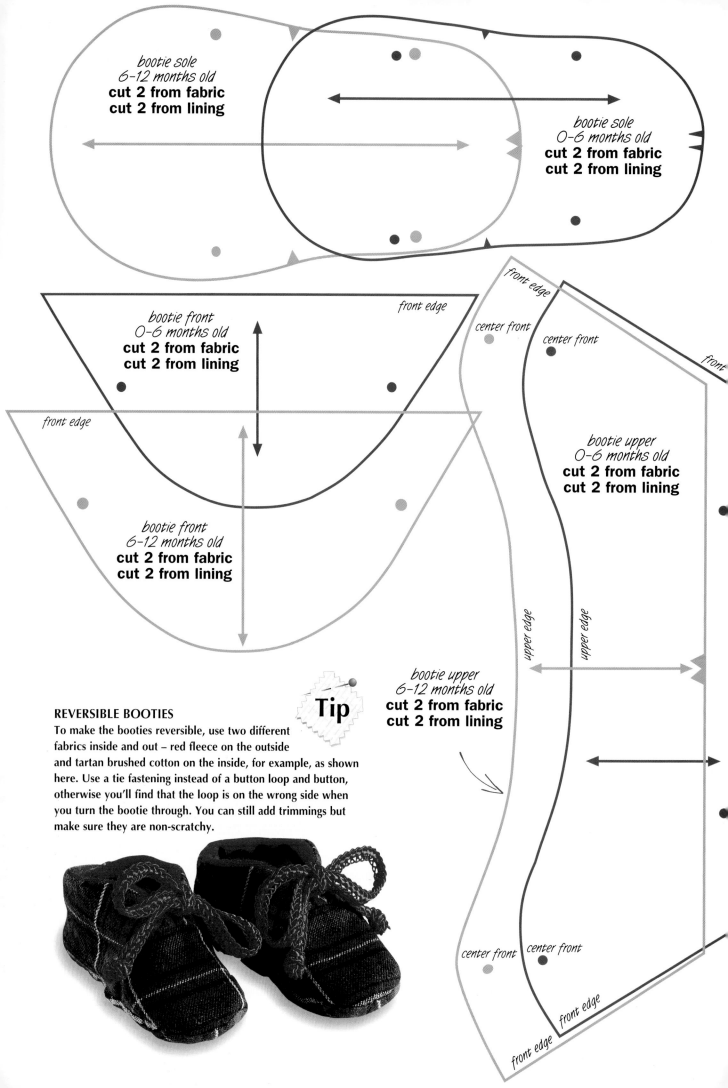

Cross stitch on clothes

*The waste-canvas method enables you to work cross stitch
on almost any fabric. Select from the library of pictorial motifs
and embroider directly on to plain baby clothes.*

Children will love these pretty little motifs – many based on cute animal characters. Use them to trim individual items of clothing, such as socks or T-shirts, or coordinate an entire outfit by embroidering lots of motifs in different colors. Many baby clothes are very plain, so the addition of even a little decorative embroidery lifts them out of the ordinary.

Cross stitch is generally worked on evenweave fabrics on which you can count the threads. The use of waste canvas makes it possible to work cross-stitch designs on fabrics which have too fine a weave for the threads to be counted.

This gives a greater scope for working cross stitch on a wide range of fabrics.

The technique involves tacking a piece of special canvas over the area to be embroidered. The weave of the canvas acts as a guide for even stitching. When the embroidery is complete, the canvas is dampened and the threads carefully pulled out, in both directions, from beneath the embroidery.

▶ *Socks look especially cute with a motif on the turn-down cuff. There are stitching charts for this quick-to-work pair of hearts, and the rocking horse above, on page 118.*

▲ *This snug all-in-one is embellished with an enchanting rocking horse motif.*

Materials and equipment

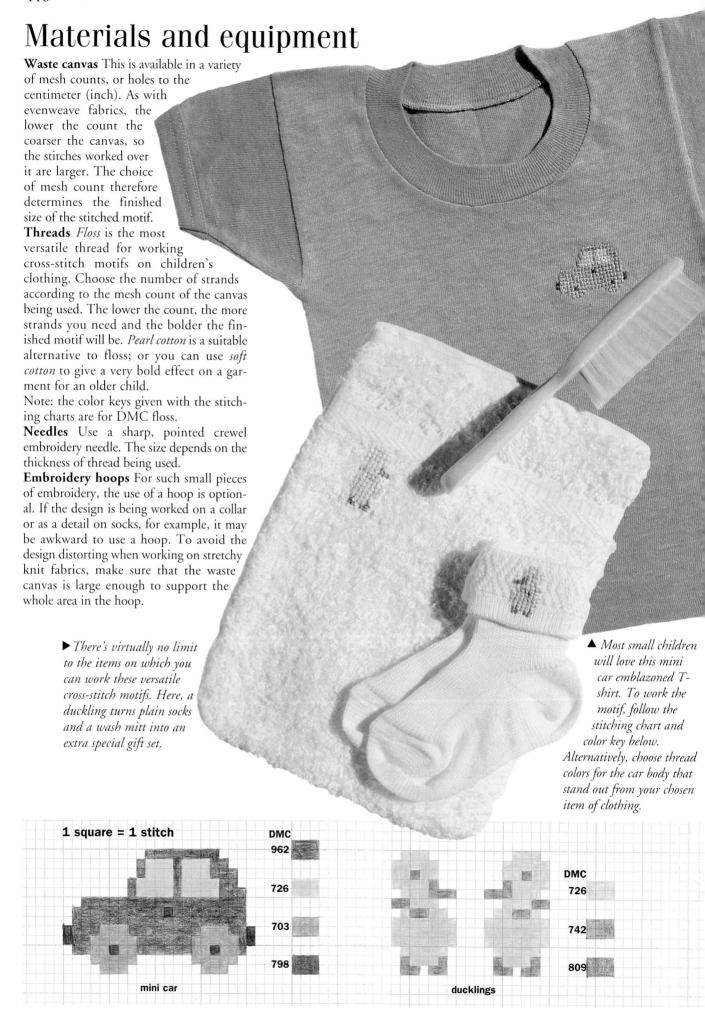

Waste canvas This is available in a variety of mesh counts, or holes to the centimeter (inch). As with evenweave fabrics, the lower the count the coarser the canvas, so the stitches worked over it are larger. The choice of mesh count therefore determines the finished size of the stitched motif.

Threads *Floss* is the most versatile thread for working cross-stitch motifs on children's clothing. Choose the number of strands according to the mesh count of the canvas being used. The lower the count, the more strands you need and the bolder the finished motif will be. *Pearl cotton* is a suitable alternative to floss; or you can use *soft cotton* to give a very bold effect on a garment for an older child.

Note: the color keys given with the stitching charts are for DMC floss.

Needles Use a sharp, pointed crewel embroidery needle. The size depends on the thickness of thread being used.

Embroidery hoops For such small pieces of embroidery, the use of a hoop is optional. If the design is being worked on a collar or as a detail on socks, for example, it may be awkward to use a hoop. To avoid the design distorting when working on stretchy knit fabrics, make sure that the waste canvas is large enough to support the whole area in the hoop.

▶ *There's virtually no limit to the items on which you can work these versatile cross-stitch motifs. Here, a duckling turns plain socks and a wash mitt into an extra special gift set.*

▲ *Most small children will love this mini car emblazoned T-shirt. To work the motif, follow the stitching chart and color key below. Alternatively, choose thread colors for the car body that stand out from your chosen item of clothing.*

1 square = 1 stitch

mini car	DMC
	962
	726
	703
	798

ducklings	DMC
	726
	742
	809

Using waste canvas

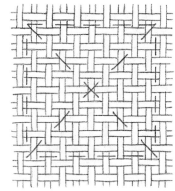

1 Attaching the waste canvas Cut a piece of waste canvas slightly larger than the motif to be stitched, or large enough to fit a hoop, if you are using one. Tack the cut piece in position on the garment, using a contrasting thread and stitching diagonally across the canvas in both directions and around the edge.

3 Removing the canvas When you have completed the design, remove the tacking threads. Place the work face up on a towel and dampen the canvas with a clean, moist cloth. When the canvas threads have softened, gently pull them out one at a time, first in one direction and then the other.

4 Pressing the embroidery Leave the embroidered fabric to dry naturally in a warm place. Then place the fabric face down on a clean, dry towel and press gently with a warm iron, taking care not to flatten the stitches.

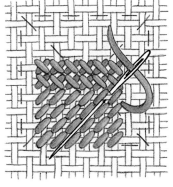

2 Stitching the motif Each colored square on the chart represents one cross stitch. Following the chart, stitch the motif using three strands of embroidery floss and forming each cross stitch over one intersection of the canvas threads.

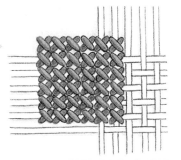

You will need

- ◆ Child's cotton T-shirt
- ◆ 12 mesh waste canvas
- ◆ Tacking thread and needle
- ◆ Crewel embroidery needle, size 8
- ◆ DMC embroidery floss (most motifs do not require a full skein)
- ◆ Small embroidery hoop, if required

Tip

COLORFASTNESS
As the canvas is dampened to remove its threads after stitching, check the embroidery floss and garment are colorfast.

▶ *Tiny motifs, such as this tow truck, make great personal logos on children's polo shirts. Follow the stitching chart and thread color key below to work the truck. After removing the canvas threads, work the pick-up hook in tiny back stitches in DMC 977.*

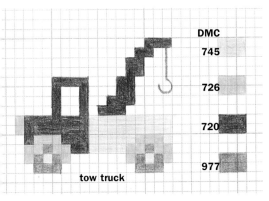

	DMC
	745
	726
	720
	977

tow truck

Pattern library

With this library of dainty cross-stitch motifs you're bound to find one that suits your taste and project. All the motifs are worked over one intersection of thread, using three strands of embroidery floss and following the instructions given on page 117. The color key is only a reference – adapt the colors as you like to suit your project.

1 square = 1 stitch

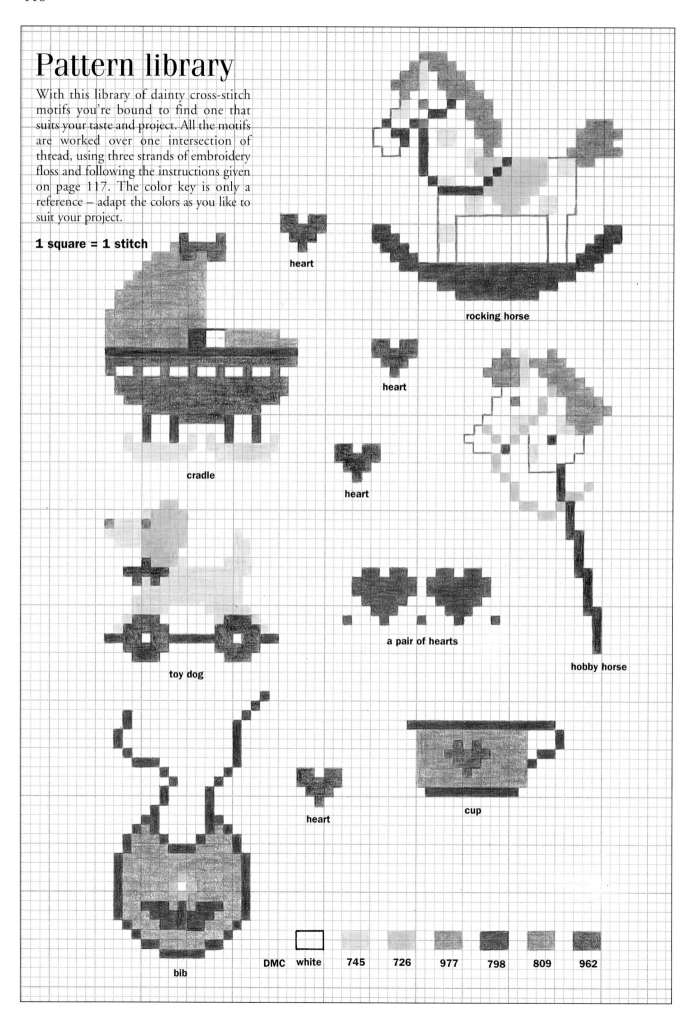

heart

rocking horse

cradle

heart

heart

toy dog

a pair of hearts

hobby horse

bib

heart

cup

| DMC | white | 745 | 726 | 977 | 798 | 809 | 962 |

Lined Moses basket

*One of the most convenient and attractive ways of carrying
a very young sleeping baby around is in a snug, draughtproof
Moses basket with a pretty padded lining.*

A lined Moses basket is an ideal and inexpensive solution for transporting small babies who mostly like to sleep a great deal while being disturbed as little as possible. It makes a delightful welcoming gift for a first baby or grandchild – either your own or a friend's.

Unlined woven rush Moses baskets are not hard to find in a variety of stores. They can vary greatly in size, so measure the dimensions carefully in order to make your own pattern for the separate pieces.

The lining is trimmed with a bound-edged single frill and attached securely to the basket with ribbon ties. Dress cottons or polyester/cottons are the most suitable fabrics to use as they are soft and lightweight, always look fresh,

▲ *Sweet dreams are assured when a baby is tucked into the cosy comfort and safety of a prettily lined Moses basket.*

and are easy to launder. They also come in a wide range of striped and floral patterns to suit any nursery theme. When you have made the lining, you can use matching or coordinating fabrics to make bedding to team up with it.

Making the lining

This lining is made from three fabrics – the main fabric seen inside the basket, a contrast fabric for the backing and another for the frill. The lining is slightly gathered on to the backing for a soft effect. The handles are also covered with a contrast fabric, but you could leave them uncovered if you prefer. The amounts given are for 140cm (54in) wide fabric.

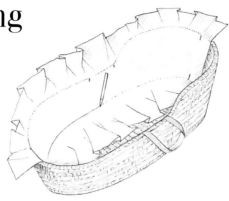

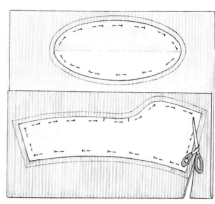

1 Making the base pattern Place a sheet of paper in bottom of basket and draw around outline of base, marking center of both head and foot ends. Remove paper and fold it in half lengthways through the two marked points. Cut out folded pattern through the two layers to get an even outline.

2 Making the side pattern On the inside of the basket, lay a piece of paper against one side wall, from the center of the head end to the center of the foot end. Mark in the top and base edges of the side section and the position for the handle. Cut out around the outline.

3 Cutting out the backing *For base:* cut one piece from backing fabric, adding a 1.5cm (⅝in) seam allowance all round. *For sides:* fold remaining fabric in two, pin side pattern on top and cut through both layers, adding a 1.5cm (⅝in) seam allowance all round. Transfer markings for handle positions.

▼ *For a really pretty, coordinated set, buy enough of the same striped and floral fabrics to line the Moses basket and make the play quilt – mixing and matching them for different effects.*

You will need

- ◆ Woven rush baby basket
- ◆ 1m (1⅛yd) cotton fabric for lining
- ◆ 30cm (⅓yd) contrast fabric for frill
- ◆ 80cm (⅞yd) contrast fabric for backing
- ◆ 20cm (¼yd) contrast fabric for handles (optional)
- ◆ 4.5m (5yd) satin bias binding
- ◆ 2.5m (2¾yd) narrow ribbon
- ◆ Large sheets of newspaper or brown paper
- ◆ Pencil
- ◆ Dressmaker's pencil

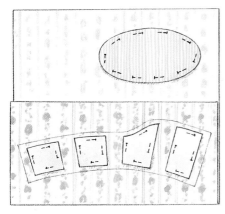

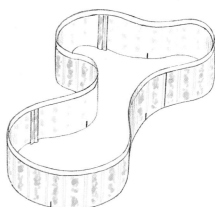

4 **Cutting out lining** *For base:* use backing base as a pattern to cut one piece from lining fabric. Fold remaining fabric in half. *For sides:* to allow for extra fullness, cut paper side pattern into four equal sections. Lay them 10cm (4in) apart on folded lining fabric. Use a dressmaker's pencil to mark an extra 5cm (2in) at head and foot ends, plus a 1.5cm (⅝in) seam allowance all round. Cut out through both layers.

5 **Making up the backing** Right sides together, pin and then stitch the two side pieces at the head and foot ends. Press seams open. Then, right sides together, match the seams to the marks on the backing base piece. Pin the bottom edge of the sides to the base and stitch in place. Mark the center of each side along the top raw edge.

6 **Making the frill** Cut three 9cm (3½in) wide strips across the width of the chosen frill fabric. Right sides together, stitch all the frill pieces together to form a loop. Neaten one long edge of the frill loop with bias binding. Fold the loop into four equal sections and mark along the raw edge.

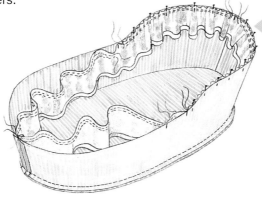

7 **Attaching the frill** Stitch two rows of gathering along raw edge of frill, 6mm (¼in) and 1cm (⅜in) in; stop and start at each mark and leave loose threads at ends for gathering. Matching raw edges and marks, pin wrong side of frill to right side of backing. Pull up gathers, pin in place and stitch, leaving openings for handles between marks on each side. Turn backing through to right side so that the frill is on the outside.

8 **Making up the lining** With right sides and raw edges together, stitch the side pieces together at the head and foot ends. Divide the lower edge into quarters and stitch two rows of gathering around each quarter, as in step **7** above.

9 **Adding the lining base** Divide base edge into quarters. Right sides together, match raw edges and marks on base and side edges. Even out gathers, pin and then stitch around base.

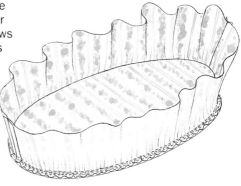

10 **Joining lining and backing** Divide lining into quarters, by using the seams at the head and foot ends and dividing the top side edge of lining in half; mark with pins and gather as in step **7**. With right sides together, match the raw edges, marks and seams on top edges of lining and backing. Pull up gathers, then pin and stitch together, sandwiching the frill between and leaving an opening on each side for handles.

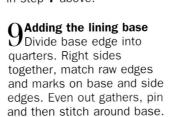

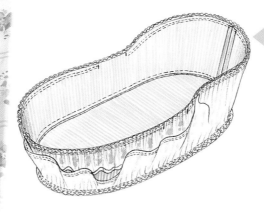

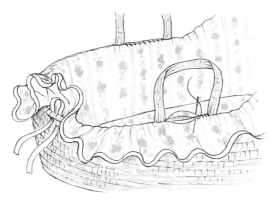

11 Adding ties Turn the lining right side out through one of the openings for the handles and push the lining down into the backing. Cut the ribbon into two equal lengths. Fold each piece in half and stitch through the fold into the backing, just below the frill, at the foot and head ends.

12 Attaching the lining to basket Position the lining in the basket, slipping the handles between the lining and frill at openings. Slipstitch the seam between the handles, turning in raw edges and catching the frill in between. Thread ends of each tie through weave of basket and tie in a bow to secure.

13 Covering the handles From contrast fabric, cut two strips the width of handle plus 2cm (¾in) by twice the length. Press under 1cm (⅜in) on each long edge and at both ends. Wrap a strip around each handle; slipstitch folded edges together along length, ruching it as you go to give a gathered effect.

Making the play quilt

Make this simple patchwork play quilt as the perfect partner to the baby's snug carry cot. It is lightly padded and lined with practical terry cloth, then edged with a contrasting border. The finished size of the quilt is 98cm (38½in) square. Amounts given below are for 140cm (54in) wide fabrics. Take 1cm (⅜in) seam allowances throughout, unless stated otherwise.

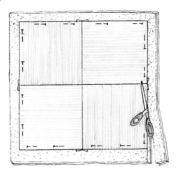

1 Making the patchwork From each striped fabric, cut two 50cm (19¾in) squares. Right sides together, join two pairs of contrasting squares. Press seams open. Stitch pairs together, with fabrics alternating. Press seam open.

2 Adding the batting and terry cloth Lay the batting on the terry cloth, and then the patchwork on top, right side up. Pin together; trim the batting and terry cloth to the size of the patchwork. Tack together at edges.

3 Cutting border Cut a strip of paper 100 x 22cm (39½ x 8¾in); this includes a 1cm (⅜in) seam allowance. Fold the strip of paper in half lengthways. At each end of the strip, fold in the short edges to meet the center fold, and trim off these triangles. Open out the paper pattern and use it to cut four pieces from the border fabric.

You will need

♦ **50cm (⅝yd) each of two contrasting striped fabrics**

♦ **1m (1⅛yd) floral fabric**

♦ **1m (1⅛yd) terry cloth**

♦ **1m (1⅛yd) lightweight batting**

♦ **Sheets of paper**

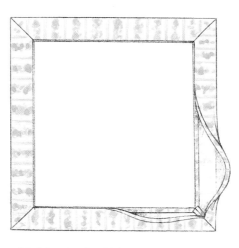

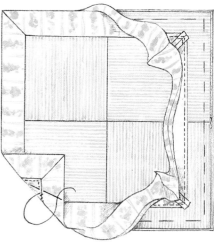

4 Joining border Right sides together, join angled ends of border strips to make a loop, starting and stopping 1cm (⅜in) from each side edge. Snip across points; press seams open. Turn to right side and push points out. Press along fold; then press 1cm (⅜in) to wrong side along raw edges. Mark center of each side with a pin.

5 Adding the border Right sides together, position folded edges of one side of border 9cm (3½in) in from edges of patchwork. Pin and stitch along foldlines. Snip into seam allowances at corners, just inside stitching. Fold border to back to enclose all the layers and slipstitch to seamline.

Windmill patchwork

*Cheerful windmills make a lively patchwork quilted panel.
It can be hung on the wall or used as a cot quilt – either
way it will brighten up the nursery or any other room.*

A toy windmill on a stick spinning in the breeze is a cheerful sight. Here is a simple machine-stitched patchwork block which uses this traditional motif to eye-catching effect. When repeated it forms a lively pattern suitable for this quilt, which makes a beautiful wall hanging. Equally, it is just the right size for a cot quilt. The quilt is finished with an intriguing border of folded triangles, called Prairie Points, that give a three-dimensional effect.

Matching tie-on seat and back pads for a favorite chair complete the set for a well coordinated bedroom or nursery. Make it in shades to suit the recipient's taste and color scheme, whether that's pastels as shown here, nursery colors or bright primaries.

▼ *Symmetrical without being static, the windmill motif makes a lively pattern for patchwork. The quilt looks good enough to hang from a peg rail rather like a tapestry and you could also make a chair seat and back pad to complete the set.*

Windmill blocks

Each windmill block measures 15cm (6in) square and uses two fabrics, including the background fabric. All the cutting measurements include a 7.5mm (¼in) seam allowance.

Use a rotary cutter, cutting mat and quilter's ruler, and always lay the pieces back in place between each step of the construction to avoid mistakes.

You will need

- 150cm (1⅝yd) background fabric
- 80cm (⅞yd) sashing fabric
- 30cm (⅜yd) of each of six other fabrics
- 120cm (1⅜yd) backing fabric
- 110 x 90cm (43 x 35in) of 50g (2oz) washable polyester batting
- Pins and basting thread
- Tacking thread
- Invisible nylon thread for quilting (optional)

Cutting out the windmill block

For **1**: *From background fabric:* cut two 10cm (3⅞in) squares. Cut each square once diagonally to give four triangles.

For **2**: *From background fabric:* cut one 11cm (4¼in) square. Cut across on both diagonals to give four small triangles.

For **3**: *From contrast fabric:* cut one 11cm (4¼in) square. Cut across on both diagonals to give four small triangles.

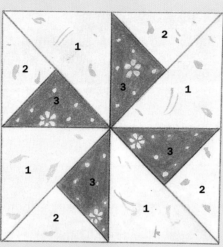

Stitching the windmill block

1 **Stitching the small triangles** Right sides together, place a triangle **2** on top of a triangle **3**. Stitch seam. Repeat with the other three pairs of **2** and **3**.

2 **Adding the large triangles** Right sides together, pin a **2-3** triangle to a large triangle **1**. Stitch to form a square. Open out the square, press seam allowances to one side and trim off protruding corners. Repeat to form three more squares and lay in position.

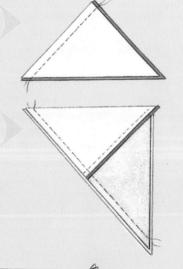

3 **Joining the squares** Stitch the squares together in pairs, checking that the pattern is correct. Then stitch the pairs together to form the block. Press.

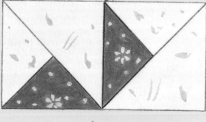

Making the quilt

The quilt uses 12 windmill blocks. The finished quilt, with sashing and borders added, measures 100 x 81cm (40 x 32in).

In addition to background and sashing fabrics, choose six other fabrics which contrast with the background and sashing. The fabric quantities are for fabric 112cm (44in) wide. They are enough for the chair seat and back pad as well as the quilt. Instructions for these are on page 126.

1 **Cutting out** *For the windmill blocks:* cut enough pieces for 12 blocks, two of each contrast fabric. *For the sashing:* from sashing fabric, cut eight strips 16.5 x 5.5cm (6½ x 2in), five strips 54.5 x 5.5cm (21½ x 2in), and two strips 81.5 x 5.5cm (32 x 2in). *For the first border:* from background fabric, cut two strips 62.5 x 6.5cm (24½ x 2½in) and two strips 91.5 x 6.5cm (36 x 2½in). *For the second border:* cut two strips 72.5 x 6.5cm (28½ x 2½in), and two strips 101.5 x 6.5cm (40 x 2½in). *For the binding:* from the sashing fabric, cut four strips 3cm (1¼in) wide across the full width of the fabric. *For the Prairie Points:* from the six contrast fabrics, cut a total of 36 9cm (3½in) squares.

2 Laying out the windmill blocks

Following the instructions on page 124, make up 12 windmill blocks. Lay them out with the design facing the same way and the colors distributed evenly.

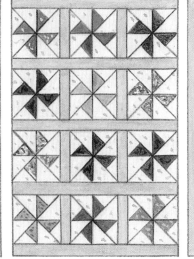

▲ *Triangular Prairie Points echo the shape of the windmill blocks and repeat the various fabrics used. A subtle background material unifies the different pattern motifs.*

Tip

SASHING SUCCESS
To fit the horizontal sashing strips accurately, finger press a crease in the center of each strip. Match the crease to the middle of the central windmill. Ease the strip in each direction to fit the row. Repeat the process for the long vertical strips.

3 Adding the sashing

Join each row of three blocks with two short sashing strips. Join the rows with the 54.5cm (21½in) strips, and add another strip the same length top and bottom. Add a long sashing strip to each side.

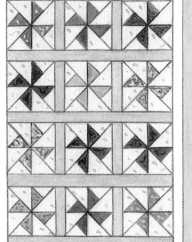

4 Stitching the first border

Stitch the shorter first border strips to the top and bottom of the quilt, matching center of strip to center of the quilt. Add the long side strips.

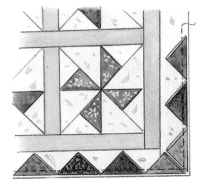

5 Adding the Prairie Points

Fold each 9cm (3½in) square on the diagonal, then fold again to make small triangles. With open sides of triangles facing the same way and right sides together, tack eight triangles to top and bottom and 10 triangles to each side of the quilt. Start 7.5mm (¼in) from the corners, with raw edges matching and tips of corner triangles touching.

6 Adding second border

Stitch second border as in step **4**, stitching through all layers including Prairie Points. Remove tacking and press seam allowance towards the center of the quilt so Prairie Points lie flat pointing outwards.

7 Finishing the quilt

On a hard, flat surface, tack the quilt top, batting and backing fabric together, using either needle and thread or nickel-plated steel safety pins. Take care not to overstretch any of the layers or the finished quilt will not lie flat. With invisible nylon thread, stitch-in-the-ditch (stitch in the indentation of a previously stitched seam) round each windmill. Then machine quilt the seam line at the base of the Prairie Point triangles to keep them lying flat.

8 Adding the binding

Stitch the binding strips to the edges of the quilt. Remove all tacking threads.

Making the chair seat and back pad

The tie-on chair back and seat pad echo the design of the quilt. For comfort, they are more thickly batted than the quilt. The seat pad measures 40cm (16in) square, and the back pad 59 x 40cm (23½ x 16in).

The fabric quantities listed for the quilt are enough for the chair pads too, and you will also need 80cm (⅞yd) of 100g (4oz) washable polyester batting, and 2.5m (2¾yd) satin ribbon for the ties.

Cut out and make up three windmill blocks in different fabrics as described on page 124.

Making the seat pad

1 Cutting out *From sashing fabric:* cut two strips 16.5 x 5.5 cm (6½ x 2in), and two strips 24.5 x 5.5cm (9½ x 2in). *From background fabric:* cut two strips 24.5 x 9cm (9½ x 3½in) and two strips 39.5 x 9cm (15½ x 3½in).

2 Sashing and border Stitch short sashing strips to opposite sides of the block. Stitch the remaining two sashing strips to the other two sides. Stitch border strips in the same way.

3 Quilting the pad Cut a square of batting to size and tack to patchwork. Stitch-in-the-ditch round windmill and outer edge of sashing strips. Remove tacking.

4 Finishing the pad Lay quilted square on a second square of batting and place these on backing fabric cut to size. Tack through all layers. Cut binding strips 4cm (1½in) wide and stitch as for quilt.

▲ *As the seat pad is plainer than the quilt – it does not have Prairie Points – it looks particularly good on a chair that is ornamented itself, perhaps, as here, shaped with curving rails. The ensemble looks extra smart when the fabric picks up the chair color.*

Making the back pad

1 Cutting out *From sashing fabric:* cut three strips 16.5 x 5.5cm (6½ x 2in), and two strips 43.5 x 5.5cm (17 x 2in). *From background fabric:* cut two strips 24.5 x 9cm (9½ x 3½in), and two strips 58.5 x 9cm (23 x 3½in).

2 Stitching the sashing and border Join the two blocks with a short sashing strip. Add another short strip at the top and bottom. Add long sashing strips to each side. Add border strips to the top and bottom then the sides as before.

3 Finishing the pad Quilt and finish the pad in the same way as the seat pad.

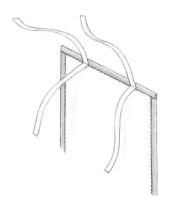

4 Adding the ties Cut the ribbon into four equal lengths and fold each piece in half. Handstitch two folded pieces of ribbon to top edge of each pad and tie to chair.

INDEX

Page numbers in *italic* refer to captions and illustrations

PICTURE ACKNOWLEDGMENTS

Photographs: CPi 99-110; Eaglemoss Publications 75(c), (Paul Bricknell) 37, 47(b), (Tony Chau) 41(l), 76(c), (Alex James) 81(l), 83(c), (Heinz Lautenbacher) 33(c), (Liz McCauley) 49(c), 50(t), 52(t), (Gloria Nichol) 77(l), 79(tr), 80(b), (Lizzie Orme) 7(b), 8(b), 9(tr), 10(tr), 21(c), 22(bl,bc), 27, 35(r), 44(r), 45(b), 55, 57, 61, 81(r), 84(c), 85(c), 86(br), 87(t), 88(br), 89, 115(t), 117(br), (Graham Rae) 23(c), 25(c), 112(br), 113(b),

114(bl), (Gareth Sambidge) 91(c), 94(tr), (Steve Tanner) 71(c), 72(br), 73(r,c,bc), 111(c), (George Taylor) 13(c), 14, 16(c), 17(c), 18(c), 20(br), 51(br), 65(c), 123(c), 125(t), 126(t); IPC Syndication (Homes & Gardens) 53(c), (Marie Louise Avery/Homes & Gardens) 12(bl), (James Merrell/Homes & Gardens) 11(c); VNU Syndication 95(c), 96(b), 116(c,sp), (Ariadne Holland) 115(br), 116(tr,bl,br), (Baby & Peuter)

119(c), 120(br); Elizabeth Whiting & Associates 67(c), 68(br).

Illustrations: Eaglemoss Publications (Shelia Coulson) 78, 118(c); John Hutchinson 50, 72, 98, 120; Coral Mula 8, 14, 18, 22, 24, 28, 34, 37(t), 38(l), 40(t), 42, 46, 54, 58, 70, 62, 66, 68, 76, 79, 82, 86, 90, 93, 96, 112, 117(t), 124; Patrick Mulrey 92.